CW00501796

Wigan Pier

The facts and fictions of an enduring Music Hall joke

John Hannavy

Every attempt has been made to secure permissions for materials reproduced in this book. If there has been any oversight we will be happy to rectify the situation and a written submission should be made to the publishers.

COVER IMAGE
If the mythical Wigan Pier had existed, this is just the sort of postcard Bamforth & Company would have published. © Bamforth & Company, reproduced by permission.

TITLE PAGE IMAGE
Two men standing on Wigan Pier, a postcard from the mid-1920s with a fully laden Canal Transport barge moored underneath the warehouse canopy.

CONTENTS PAGE IMAGE
When the restoration of the pier area was completed in 1986 and *The Way We Were* heritage centre opened, the 'Wigan Pier' logo appeared on countless souvenirs, including books, badges and fridge magnets and yes, there actually were sticks of Wigan Pier rock.

Images from the following photographers and collections are acknowledged with thanks: Bamforth & Company cover, 86 *top right*, 136 *top*; Anthony Grimshaw 25 *top*, 28 *bottom left*, 33 *bottom*, 38 *top*; © National Railway Museum/SSPL 72 *top*; David and Marilyn Parkinson 98 *top*, 124 *top left;* Andy Skilling 141 *bottom;* photographs by Arnold Hall, Jack Winstanley Collection, 36, 39 *top*; Alan Robinson 121 *middle & bottom*; Lynda Wearn 105 *top*; Greg Venables 114 *top left & right*; © Wigan Council 32, 139, 141 *top*

It has proved impossible to locate the current owners of a number of the images from which I made copies thirty years ago, but I trust I have not over-stepped the mark by reproducing them here.

All other images were taken by the author or come from the John Hannavy Image Library.
©1969-2016 John Hannavy.

Thanks to Jack Winstanley; Ian Wallace of Bamforth & Company; Lynda Wearn; Andy Skilling; Greg Venables; Sue Harper, 48th Fighter Wing Public Affairs, USAF; Bill Millard who loaned me family photographs in 1985; Wigan Planning Officers Steve Thomson and Steve Burns; Lynda Jackson and Alex Miller at Wigan Archives and Museum Services; David and Marilyn Parkinson, Chris Scobie; Anthony Grimshaw; and Geoffrey Shryhane.

The lyrics of Jack Winstanley's *Ballad of Wigan Pier* are reproduced courtesy of Jack Winstanley.
Extracts from Arthur Munby's diaries are reproduced courtesy of the Master and Fellows of Trinity College Cambridge.
The extract from the *Manchester Guardian* is © the Guardian Media Group.
Extracts from *The Road To Wigan Pier* by George Orwell (Copyright © George Orwell, 1937) are reprinted by permission of Bill Hamilton as the Literary Executor of the Estate of the Late Sonia Brownell Orwell.
Extracts from *On The Wigan Boat Express*, Words & Music by George Formby, Harry Gifford & Frederick Cliffe, © Copyright Lawrence Wright Music Co Ltd. Chester Music Limited trading as Campbell Connelly & Co., and Sony/ATV Music Publishing, EMI Music Publishing. All Rights Reserved. International Copyright Secured. Used by Permission of Chester Music Limited trading as Campbell Connelly & Co.
Extracts from *Wigan Pier*, Words & Music by Robert Weston & Bert Lee, © Sony/ATV Music Publishing, EMI Music Publishing.
The cover of Jasper Fforde's *Well of Lost Plots* is © Hodder Paperbacks.

Published by LIGHTMOOR PRESS
© Lightmoor Press & John Hannavy 2016
Designed by John Hannavy
(www.johnhannavy.co.uk)

British Library Cataloguing-in-Publication Data. A catalogue record for this book is available from the British Library
ISBN: 9781911038 13 9
All rights reserved. No part of this publication may be reproduced, stored in a retrieval system or transmitted in any form or by any means, electronic, mechanical, photocopying, recording or otherwise, without the written permission of the publisher.

LIGHTMOOR PRESS
Unit 144B, Lydney Trading Estate, Harbour Road, Lydney, Gloucestershire GL15 5EJ
www.lightmoor.co.uk
Lightmoor Press is an imprint of Black Dwarf Lightmoor Publications Ltd

Printed in England by Henry Ling Ltd, The Dorset Press, Dorchester
www.henryling.co.uk

CONTENTS

TO THE PIER

INTRODUCTION

THE VERY IDEA OF WIGAN PIER is an engaging one, and working on a project like this can only be described as 'great fun'. George Formby Senior would, I am sure, have approved of that fun. Just who was responsible for Wigan Pier's 'creation' will never be known, but still the idea endures that there may once have been a mythical seaside pier in the middle of industrial Lancashire.

As with any book, the author is, in many ways, simply the compiler – the one who draws together other people's knowledge and ideas, adds his own interpretation, and assembles the whole to create the story. While I am indebted to many people in Wigan for their help and support over the years, particular thanks go to Jack Winstanley with whom I co-wrote the first book on Wigan Pier thirty years ago. Looking again at the film *Wigan Pier – Myth to Reality* which we made together for BBC television in 1986, it seems like almost a lifetime ago! The lyrics of Jack's delightful *Ballad of Wigan Pier* are reproduced with his permission.

Continued research over the past thirty years into the stories of the pier has revealed much new material, and the fruits of that research underpins this new book.

This project started out as a search for the Holy Grail – George Formby Senior's *Wigan Pier* scripts – but they probably never existed, although I am still looking!

2016 marks two important anniversaries – it is 200 years since the completion of the Leeds to Liverpool Canal in 1816, and probably 125 years since the first stories were told about Wigan Pier.

When I first arrived in Wigan in the autumn of 1969 to take up my first teaching appointment as the lecturer in charge of photography in the wonderfully named Wigan & District Mining & Technical College – now with the more prosaic title of Wigan & Leigh College – the rich history of Wigan Pier, the myth, the jokes and the town's burden by association with the 'Wigan Pier' of George Orwell's famous book were all unfamiliar to me.

I soon became engrossed in the story, not least because wherever I travelled in Britain and told people that I lived

opposite: When *The Way We Were* heritage centre at Wigan Pier first opened in 1986, visitors were directed into the exhibition by a large image of the project's first 'Piermaster', Peter Lewis, and his deputy Hazel Hawarden, in the style of a typical seaside entertainment with cut-out holes through which holidaymakers would poke their heads to be photographed by an Edwardian beach photographer.

inset: The canalside buildings looking towards the now-demolished Pier Nightclub and the replica 'Wigan Pier'.

below: The author, *right*, photographed with Jack Winstanley at Wigan Pier in March 1986 during the filming of the BBC tv programme.

THE PIER, WIGAN.
801.

in Wigan, the response would be a sniggering utterance of those two words which perennially cursed the town – 'Wigan Pier' – usually by people who had never visited Wigan themselves, knew nothing of the richness of its history and didn't know much about the jokes either!

In the forty-seven years since I first arrived – thirty-seven of them living in and around the town – I have watched the local council's attitude to the pier and all its accompanying baggage change several times.

In 1986, Wigan Pier's past as a civic embarrassment was consigned to its own little corner of history and replaced by justifiable civic satisfaction at a remarkable rebirth. Generations of deeply held sensitivity towards being the persistent butt of a Victorian joke were replaced by a justified swagger. The town's past was no longer to be ignored, no longer to be sniggered about – it was to be celebrated. When that change came about, the once-derelict area of the town around the canal basin all-too-briefly blossomed as one of the north-west's 'must visit' tourist attractions, and a wonderful showcase for the town's considerable and important industrial heritage – coal and cotton primarily – as well as the indomitable resilience of the working people who made Wigan famous.

The first ever book on the pier – *Wigan Pier: An Illustrated History* – which I co-wrote with Jack Winstanley, former editor of the *Wigan Observer*, was published in 1985 to coincide with the regeneration of the pier area.

In early 1986, Jack and I explored the pier and canalside while being followed by BBC television cameras for the documentary *Wigan Pier – myth to reality*, broadcast on the evening of the Royal Visit when Her Majesty the Queen opened the Wigan Pier Heritage Centre.

Fast forward thirty years, and the area is once again the subject of a dilemma. The museum of Wigan's industrial history which was housed in one of the 19th century canalside warehouses – *The Way We Were* – has been closed since 2007; the electric waterbuses no longer glide along the canal

opposite page: The replica Wigan Pier, floodlit on the evening before the Royal Visit in 1986. When first built in 1845, it was known as the Pier Head at Wigan.

inset: Locals posing on Bankes's coal tippler, from a postcard c.1920.

below: This gently humorous postcard, published c.1910, reminded mill workers that their Wigan accent was recognisable pretty much anywhere they went on holiday – not that many of them ever ventured further than Southport or Blackpool.

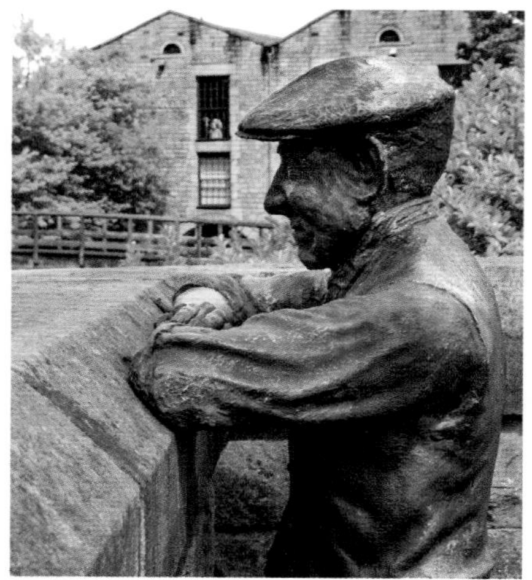

Wigan Council commissioned a set of four sculptures which recalled the town's past industries, to be set up around the Pier in 2009. They depicted a bargee, a boat-builder, a pit brow lass and a mill girl. Before they were officially unveiled, they had been vandalised. The makers were called back to reinforce two of the figures, and the bargee, *here*, had the top of his head sliced off and a metal pole inserted down into the ground before he was then filled with concrete and the top of his head glued back on. The pit brow lass disappeared shortly afterwards but has since been put back near the replica pier.

between the Heritage Centre and Trencherfield Mill, and the replica of the coal tippler which became known as Wigan Pier stands alongside graffiti-daubed walls, its wooden platform slowly succumbing to the elements and rotting away. Plans to replace it with a fully working replica never came to fruition. Trencherfield's great steam engine is still fired up on occasional Sundays and its distinctive hooter still welcomes visitors but in fewer numbers than once marvelled at its size and power.

Efforts to reverse that decline are underway. Once again there are plans to regenerate the area – this time as 'The Wigan Pier Quarter' – but in the present economic climate, development progress is understandably slow.

Wigan Pier: An Illustrated History was my fourth book on the town and, having lived there for only sixteen years, I was still considered a relative newcomer, a foreigner, an interloper. Luckily, Jack Winstanley's local pedigree was much more robust than mine and my appreciation of Jack's friendship – and both his research and journalistic skills – remains undiminished. We also enjoyed two years teaching together on a pioneering editorial design course at the college.

In 2003, when my eighth book on Wigan was published – after thirty-four years living and working there – my Scottish roots and lack of local pedigree still undermined my credentials as a local historian.

There was even a post on a local website, by a 'Wiganer' complaining that I had no right to be *'setting myself up'* as qualified to write about *'his'* town – posted by someone who had only just been born when my first book on Wigan's history was published.

Perhaps he was right, as being a Wiganer has everything to do with being born in Wigan, of Wigan stock, rather than anything as irrelevant as how long one might have happened to live in the town. My son, born and raised in Wigan, probably doesn't even really qualify either.

left: The earliest tinted postcard of the canal basin yet discovered – dating from c.1902 – makes no mention of Wigan Pier whatsoever, referring to the area as 'Canal Wharf, Wigan'. To the right is Bridge 59 – *see pages 12-13*. This is one of the earliest cards produced by Will Smith who published more than a hundred different postcards of the town and its people – many of them tinted and printed in Saxony – between 1900 and the early 1930s. They were widely available throughout the area.

Despite moving away from the area in 2006, I had not allowed for my enduring fascination with the impact which this late-Victorian flight-of-fancy – an off-the-cuff 'one-liner' later picked up and developed by a Music Hall comedian – could have both nationally and internationally, its echoes still resounding through generations and across continents.

Returning to Wigan to start work on this project just eight years later, I found a town already changed dramatically – and even more dramatic changes to both the town centre and the Wigan Pier Quarter are planned over the next few years.

But the Pier's fame and infamy – perhaps in equal measure – still resonate with and appeal to people well beyond the geographical boundaries of the old County Borough.

below left: Will Smith's newsagents and tobacconist shop on Wigan Lane, from an advertisement c.1920, with the windows displaying just a selection of the many postcards of the town and its environs which he published.

THE
ORWELL
BARS & RESTAURANT
THE
ORWELL
AT
WIGAN PIE

Wigan Pier has certainly had a rich and colourful past – in both fact and fiction – and while the fictional, mythical, Wigan Pier remains elusive, and the structure which inspired it seems, frustratingly, to have been undocumented, only the coming years will reveal whether or not the area around the iconic industrial symbol that has long been known as 'Wigan Pier' can preserve that history and have a sustainable future.

I hope that the wealth of new information about the history and legacy of the pier, and the songs and jokes forever associated with it that are contained in this book, fittingly mark 2016's two anniversaries.

It is also to be hoped that it helps in some small way to enhance and preserve Wigan Pier's place in the town's fascinating history as the canalside area faces its most radical redevelopment in more than two hundred years.

John Hannavy 2016

opposite page: In the years since *The Way We Were* closed its doors, its content put into store, *The Orwell*, seen here on a still winter morning, has stood alone, much of its passing visitor trade gone along with the electric waterbuses which once tied up at the key adjacent to it. This once-thriving venue succumbed to the dearth of customers and closed its doors – hopefully temporarily – at the end of 2014.

Above: From the 'Ja-Ja Heraldic Series' of Edwardian postcards, a gilded reproduction of the town's coat of arms.

left: A still spring day in early 2001, looking down towards the Heritage Centre Shop and Education Building – the 1774 warehouse – with the Orwell pub beyond.

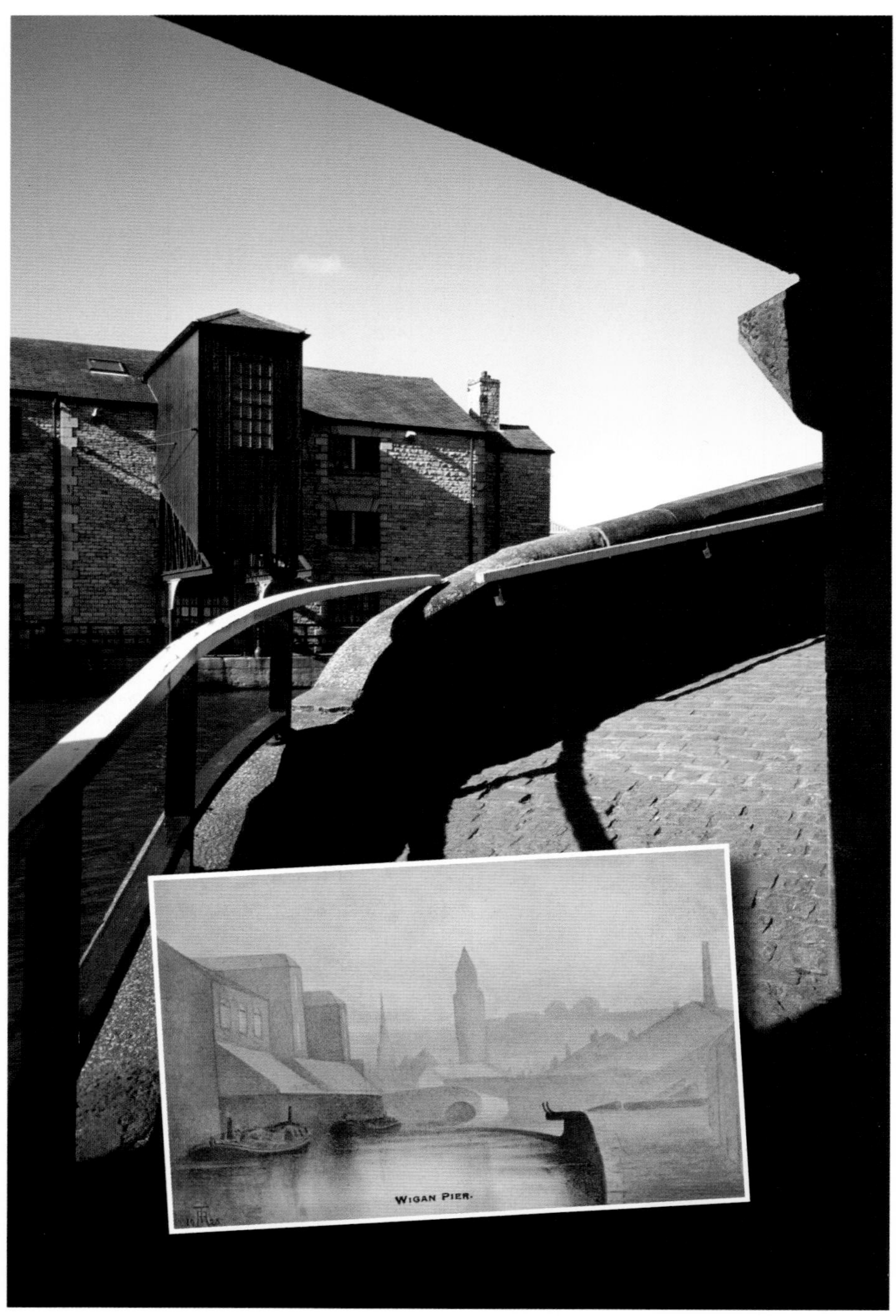
WIGAN PIER.

SETTING THE SCENE

WHEN THE TRAVEL WRITER H.V. MORTON visited Wigan in 1926 while on one of his many tours – he was writing the first of his three English travelogues, *In Search of England*, at the time, he found a town unhappy with its image. That was an image with which he believed Wigan had been unjustly saddled. He wrote:

> *'Wigan, were it not inhabited by a race of sturdy and rather tough Lancashire folk, would be the most self-conscious town in England. For years it has suffered from a joke. The words 'Wigan Pier' spoken by a comedian on a Music Hall stage are sufficient to make an audience howl with laughter, and the ease with which the name works on the sensibilities of an audience is probably, in some measure, responsible for the great success of this joke.*
>
> *Wigan, to millions of people who have never seen and never will see the town, represents the apex of the world's pyramid of gloom. So serious has the Wigan joke become that the go-ahead Corporation, who are full of local pride, take what steps they can to counteract it; but the silly old joke goes on!'*

'Certain Wigonians of high commercial standing', as Morton described the leaders of the town's industries, felt that the

opposite: Known as a 'changeline bridge', Bridge 59 at Pottery Road gave access from the Wigan Basin to the eastern section of the canal towards Leeds. This steep curved ramp enabled horses to negotiate the bridge and change from one towpath to the other while still towing their barges. Wooden rope rollers on bridge piers, were worn into grooves in the days before steam power.

inset: By the time H.V. Morton arrived in the town, Wigan Pier was celebrated on numerous postcards. This one, was based on a 1925 watercolour, *Early Morning, Wigan Pier* by Alderman Thomas Ramsden, a herbalist with a shop at 4 Makinson Arcade. Ramsden served as the town's 692nd Mayor from 1938 to 1939. The original, watercolour, just 6.5 x 9.5 inches in size, sold at auction in 2011 for £12. Some examples of this card carried an advert for Cod Liver Oil produced by Thomas Aspinall & Sons of Kenyon Road.

left: Wigan Pier in 2003 from a similar viewpoint to Ramsden's painting.

above: An Edwardian 'lovers' postcard overprinted 'at Wigan'. Versions of the same card could also be bought at those seaside resorts which actually did have pleasure piers.

below: From an Edwardian postcard, crowds of holidaymakers are seen dancing on Blackpool's Central Pier around 1910 – a scene replicated on many of the piers around England's coast. Had George Formby's mythical Wigan Pier ever existed, similar pleasures would surely have been enjoyed along its walkways.

widespread ridicule which they believed the town's name engendered brought a measurable blight on the county borough's ability to build on its already considerable commercial and industrial base. Morton, who had already travelled widely throughout England, came strongly to the town's defence:

'Now, I had been in Wigan just ten minutes when I saw that there is no joke! Wigan is a spa compared with towns like Wednesbury, in the Black Country, and with certain of the Staffordshire pottery towns. I admit frankly that I, too, shared the common idea of Wigan. I admit that I came here to write an impression of unrelieved gloom—of dreary streets and stagnant canals and white-faced Wigonians dragging their weary steps along dull streets haunted by the horror of the place in which they are condemned to live.

This is nonsense. I would not mind spending a holiday in Wigan—a short one.'

Morton's view of the town, as described in *In Search of England* was unstintingly positive, which is perhaps why he is rarely quoted.

On the other hand, the picture of the town painted in 1937 by George Orwell – Eric Blair – in *The Road to Wigan Pier* exploits the already embedded image of what Morton described as *'the apex of the world's pyramid of gloom'* to further promulgate the idea that Wigan was the archetype

A comic postcard from c.1906 showing that the new craze for amateur photography had reached seaside piers. Given the fact that a growing number of people were using cameras by the end of the 19th century, it is surprising that there were so few photographs taken of Wigan's canal at the time, and apparently none of the wooden structure which gave rise to the jokes about the pier.

and the ultimate exemplar of everything that was abhorrent about industrial England.

Orwell's writings are discussed later in this book but to understand the whole subsequent story of Wigan Pier, it is important to recognise that the scars of the image he presented continued to hurt the town and its inhabitants for much of the 20th century. That image, even now long after it ought to have been dispelled, still partly endures deep in the national psyche.

H.V. Morton would briefly return to the subject of the Wigan Pier joke in his 1929 book *In Search of Scotland*, while exploring the history of the hundreds of jokes which persist about Aberdeen and Aberdonians.

He suggested there must be a secret building in Aberdeen, built of solid granite and totally inaccessible to the general public, where the quality of jokes about the city was rigorously assessed by a committee before they were made public, in order to ensure that only the highest quality insults ever gained public notoriety. But how the two places dealt with their jokes was, he believed, fundamentally different. Perhaps Wigan needed a similar committee.

'Wigan in Lancashire and Aberdeen are two places known throughout the kingdom by virtue of a joke. When I was in Wigan the Town Clerk pleaded with me to do

main picture: Southport Pier, on the coast a few miles from Wigan, was the probable inspiration for George Formby's mythical pier. The 1,200 yard long pier opened to the public in 1860 and is the second longest seaside pier in Britain, being exceeded in length only by Southend. The first pile was driven into the sand in August 1859, with the entire construction taking almost exactly one year, so by the time the idea of Wigan's mythical pier was first mooted, Southport's cast-iron structure was already nearly forty years old. A regular train service from Wigan Wallgate to Southport had been opened five years before the pier was built, so rail travel between the two towns was already well established and Southport, like Blackpool, a regular destination for Wakes Week holidays for those who could afford them and day trips for others.

inset: Seaside Pierrots, from postcards produced in 1904 (*below*) and c.1918 (*bottom*). Had it existed, the mythical Wigan Pier would surely have had such troupes.

> *what I could to discount this joke. Aberdeen however, with its superlative sense of business, enjoys stories against Aberdeen as Jews enjoy stories against their race. This, contrary to popular belief, is the only resemblance between the two peoples. The real Aberdeen joke is, of course, the free publicity given to the city by those who spread it!'*

The town's sensitivity towards the joke was obviously very raw in the 1920s and showed no sign of lessening as the 1930s progressed. Indeed, Wigan had actually entered an era of denial, persuading itself that if no mention was made of it, the pier would, of its own accord, just go away.

And that is exactly the approach taken by John T. Hilton in the 1934 edition of his *Wigan Town and Country Rambles*, published by the Caxton Press in Rowbottom Square.

Hilton had nothing whatsoever against the idea of Wigan as a holiday resort – indeed he believed that had it not been for the adverse effects of coal mining, it might well have become just that, writing

> *'Wigan might have been a fashionable inland resort at this day had its mineral wells, which existed in many parts of the town, down to the 18th century, been developed by our ancestors. Unhappily, the Spa has been drained away by the coal mines of the district, but traces of the wells still remain in the neighbourhood of Harrogate Street. What, therefore, might have been utilised for the public good and the town's benefit, has been lost for ever.*
>
> *The waters were said to contain medicinal properties, derived from the solution of substances through which they passed. Dr. Leigh, an eighteenth century writer on medicial waters, observes that* 'the vitriol spring at the cannel pits at Haigh near Wigan when he first tried it, yielded an ounce of vitriol for a quart of water.' *He also mentions that chalybeate waters were found at Wigan and gives a full description of the burning well at Arncliffe near Wigan.'*

Perhaps having been subjected to similar entreaties from the Town Clerk who had begged Morton to do what he could to '*discount this joke*', John Hilton made no mention

Beyond repair? Several members of Wigan Borough Council believed so in 1970, and suggested the whole area be cleared and redeveloped. Many of the buildings appeared close to collapse, but when surveyed a decade later and found to be structurally sound, the idea of developing the Wigan Pier area into a tourist attraction evolved – ensuring the conservation of a major feature of the town's rich industrial heritage.

of the pier whatsoever in his book – and indeed only mentioned those scenic stretches of the canal outside the town where they run through Haigh, Gathurst and Appley Bridge.

Did Hilton recognise the irony of spa waters having been found and then lost in the area around Harrogate Street – the Yorkshire town of the same name having developed into one of England's fashionable spas while the name of Wigan became synonymous with the downside of industrialisation, poverty and hardship?

The cover of the 1934 edition of Hilton's book – the first edition of which had actually been published in Leicester twenty years earlier by the Criterion Press.

The vile-smelling sulphurous waters of the mineral springs at Haigh would, indeed, have been ideal spa waters while '*chalybeate waters*' – rich in iron and other minerals – and also present at Harrogate, were what made the spas at places such as Royal Tunbridge Wells famous.

So Wigan missed out on developing as a spa resort, becoming instead not just an industrial powerhouse but a powerhouse with its own mythical pier.

But what of Wigan Pier itself? When it was announced in 1929 that Wigan Pier was to be demolished, *The Manchester Guardian*, under the heading of 'A Wigan Fairy Tale' in its 'Miscellany' column on 7th December 1929, ridiculed the

THE
ORWELL
BARS & RESTAURANT

More than thirty years separate these two views of the former Orwell pub and restaurant and the Wigan Basin. The brick warehouse building with its cast-iron and timber goods hoist tower, opened as *The Orwell* in 1986, was built in c.1880 as Gibson's Cotton Warehouse. Connected to it is the original stone-built terminal warehouse dating from the 1770s, and probably built at the time, as work on the canal reached Wigan in 1774. The hoist tower on this building was probably added some time in the 19th century. The stone-built corn warehouse with twin barge access, to the right of the pictures, was completed around 1815. All three buildings were largely reconstructed during the restoration of the Wigan Basin area in the early 1980s. The clock tower was added to *The Orwell* in 1989-90. When the *South Lancashire* volume of Nikolaus Pevsner's monumental series of books, *The Buildings of England*, was published in 1969, the canal and its surrounding area was so derelict that it received not a mention. By the 2006 second edition, it was considered worthy of inclusion – a reflection of changing attitudes towards 18th and 19th century industrial architecture. *inset:* The canal basin as it looked in 1970.

top: The 19th century warehouses in the canal basin near Wigan Pier as they looked in the early spring of 1970, just a few months after the author moved to the town.

above: Fifteen years later, with restoration work on the canalside buildings nearing completion, the floodlights were tested for the first time.

very idea that such a thing might even be possible, commenting that it was:

> *'rather like announcing that four o'clock tomorrow afternoon is to be thoroughly overhauled and painted green.*
>
> *What do they know of Wigan Pier who say it can be dismantled? You might as well talk about spring-cleaning a rainbow or arresting the Wandering Jew for loitering without visible means of support.*
>
> *The realists, it appears, consider that Wigan Pier is* 'an iron structure which had been used for about half a century for tipping coal wagons from an adjacent colliery on to canal boat' *and it is that structure which is now to be pulled down. Only a coarse and essentially commonplace mind would accept a story of that kind. The real – that is to say, the transcendental and ineffable – Wigan Pier is a mighty different sort of affair whose dwelling is the 'high, windless world and strange' celebrated by Rupert Brooke in a sonnet on platonic idealism. In other words, it is a deathless resident in the realm of original ideas – it abuts on the infinite and not on any material canal.*
>
> *Let Wigan do what it likes with the fifty-year-old iron structure – the true, transcendental Wigan Pier of a thousand music hall nights is imperishable.'*

The *Wigan Observer*, which had earlier carried the original announcement, paraphrased the *Manchester Guardian* piece a week after it appeared – perhaps the first time that one of the local newspapers had ever acknowledged the existence of the immortal Music Hall fantasy.

The mythical seaside Wigan Pier is a construct which defies any sort of logic and that perhaps is a key reason for its longevity.

In a way, the subsequent celebration of the six-foot long coal tippler as 'Wigan Pier' is an essential part of the joke's endurance. Each is just as incongruous as the other.

Did locals, when asked where the pier was by visitors who knew of it only from the music halls, quietly smile to themselves – and perhaps even feel a wicked delight – as they directed those visitors to the tippler?

The difference between what they were anticipating, and their surprise and disappointment when confronted by such an insignificant structure must have been considerable. Whatever the locals may have thought, the council's attitude remained firmly rooted somewhere between discomfort with and ambivalence towards the idea for decades.

In the late 1970s, as part of a multi-faceted plan to 'relaunch' and market the 'new' Wigan, there was even a specially inaugurated postmark claiming that '*Modern Wigan has no Peer*'.

By the early 1980s, the borough had embraced the very strategy for which Morton had praised Aberdeen half a century earlier – if you can't make the jokes go away, capitalise on them and turn them to your advantage.

While the twenty-one year success of *The Way We Were* admirably proved the wisdom of that approach, the heritage project concerned itself mostly with the town's industrial past – particularly around the year 1900 at the height of the coal and iron industries but it acknowledged the jokes about the pier only briefly.

But since the heritage centre closed, the contents have languished in stores across the borough, the site slowly reverting to its earlier decay and abandonment.

The slow-moving redevelopment of the Wigan Basin and its unique collection of Victorian buildings can't come a moment too soon if the pier's future is to be assured.

below: The Terminal Warehouse in 1970 – looking 'terminal' in just about every respect – was built c.1815 by local corn merchants at what was then the eastern end of the canal. It was one of the first canal warehouses to allow the loading and unloading of barges fully under cover.

bottom: Restored in the 1980s and given the prestigious address of 'No. 1 Wigan Pier', the former grain store became high quality offices.

right: The Leeds & Liverpool Canal was once the only major transport artery in the region. First it was crossed at Gathurst by the Southport & Manchester Railway in 1855 – seen in the distance – and more than a century later by the M6 motorway. The average speed on the canal with horse-drawn barges was about 4mph. On the railway, that increased tenfold to around 40mph by the end of the 19th century, while today traffic thunders overhead on the motorway at 70.

below: A narrowboat makes its way down the Wigan flight from Top Lock in July 2015.

But the mythical Wigan Pier lives on despite all the years of neglect around the canal.

Several enterprising Wiganers, moving abroad to set up businesses far from the town, have taken the name with them – recognising that an association with the world-famous pier is a valuable sales asset for their enterprises. So, in Tenerife and in Canada – and reportedly even in Turkey – bars and restaurants can be found proudly carrying the name of Wigan

above: Wigan Basin, 1960s. A pleasure boat is moored alongside what became the Orwell public house, while dumb boats lie semi-submerged at the vaulted entrances to the grain warehouse.

below: Trencherfield Mill engine today.

Pier – not bad for something which never really existed and for an important part of the town's history which was for so long a source of civic embarrassment.

History cannot be erased, and as *The Manchester Guardian* said, '*the true, transcendental Wigan Pier of a thousand music hall nights is imperishable*'.

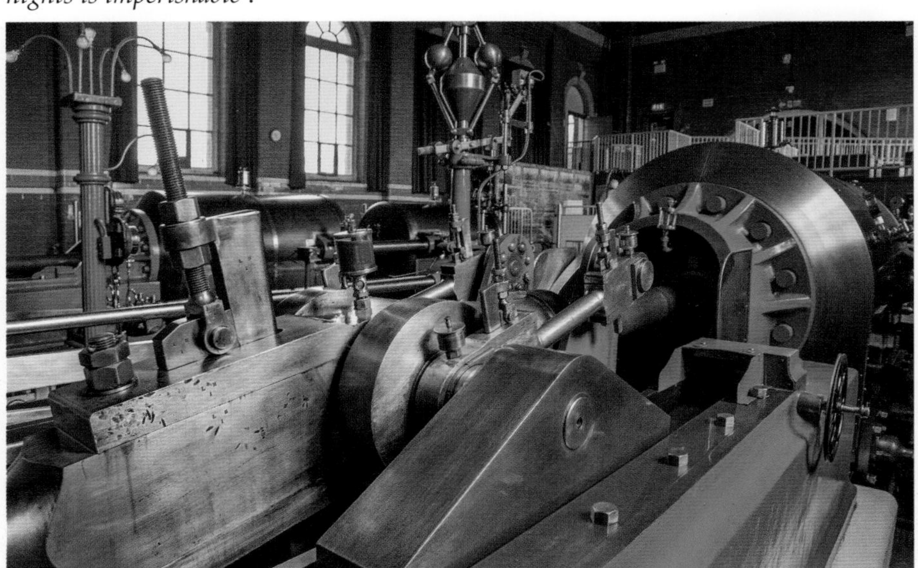

ROLAND
Registered No 5

A CUT ABOVE THE REST

THE LEEDS TO LIVERPOOL CANAL on which Wigan stands is over 120 miles long, has ninety-seven locks, rises 500 feet up and over the top of the Pennines, and took nearly fifty years to complete. Several names were proposed for the new navigation – it was originally to be known as either the Lancashire & Yorkshire Canal or the Grand Canal.

Considering that the canal was cut between 1770 and 1816, at a time when construction work was largely carried out by navvies with picks and shovels, the engineering achievement almost defies comprehension. But the canal was not the first project to open up Wigan's industries – mainly coal and iron – to a much wider market.

Building work on the canal started at a time when the only real alternative to water-transport was the horse-drawn cart – something the burghers of Wigan had already recognised earlier in the 18th century, when they had proposed an Act of Parliament to widen and dredge the stretch of the River Douglas from Newtown, a mile from Wigan town centre, to where it meets the Ribble at Hesketh Bank. Their first Bill was rejected by the House of Lords but a second one was passed in 1720, although not acted upon immediately.

opposite: Colourful reflections of a narrowboat moored on the canal just outside Wigan.

inset: For many years the restored wide-boat *Roland* stood in the gardens between Trencherfield Mill and the mill's own cutting off the canal.

above: A narrowboat approaching Bridge 57 in the 1970s.

left: The Wigan end of the Douglas Navigation, near the DW Stadium at Robin Park.

right: Dean Locks near Gathurst, south of Wigan, are today dominated by the M6 flyover. The reeds to the right mark where a lock, now filled in, once linked the canal to the Douglas Navigation, a vital trading link into Wigan until the canal reached the town. The section of canal from Liverpool to Dean Locks opened in 1774, the section to Wigan taking five more years to complete.

The movement of Wigan's vast resources of coal – and increasing demand for it well beyond the limits of easy transportation – was the prime consideration in the establishment of that first waterway, with several early 18th century colliery owners prominently named as sponsors of the project.

It took around twenty years and £20,000 – a significant sum at the time – from the passing of the Act of Parliament to the final completion of the Douglas Navigation in 1742 – most of it had opened four years earlier – by which time a succession of eighteen weirs and locks had been constructed to enable boats to sail from Miry Lane End Basin in Newtown, about a mile from Wigan town centre, to join the Ribble at Tarleton.

In Volume II of his monumental *History of Wigan*, published in 1882 by local newspaper proprietor Thomas Wall, David Spencer went into considerable detail when describing the Act of Parliament which laid the foundations for the development of the Douglas Navigation and outlined the commercial benefits its backers believed it would bring to Wigan. He made much of the sweeping rights granted by the Act to the project's backers who were, in his words:

'empowered to appropriate land belonging to the king, public, or corporate bodies or private individuals, and to remove all impediments that might hinder navigation,

below: Several bridges along the canal in and around the Wigan Basin are grooved from the rubbing of ropes as horse drawn barges were coaxed along the canal. Some were fitted with wooden rollers to avoid this wear.

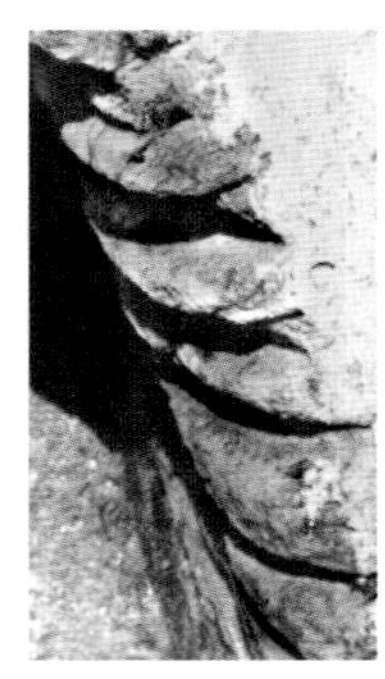

left: The canal was built with several branches – the Rufford Branch, seen here, incorporated part of the route of the Douglas Navigation.

overleaf: From Top Lock – Lock 65 – the canal makes its way downhill towards Wigan through a flight of twenty-three locks. Trade on the waterway – mainly consisting of coal and iron but many other commodities as well – was once so busy that several boats would be waiting in each of the wide lagoons for their turn to enter the next lock. Much of the cargo was being moved to and from the Wigan Coal & Iron Company's Kirkless Works near Top Lock.

inset: The 'dumb boat' *Helena* was built in 1890 for the Wigan Coal & Iron Company, probably at the company's own boatyard in Aspull near Springs Bridge. She carried coal for the company until nationalisation in 1946. She was sold to John Parke & Sons of Liverpool in 1948 and renamed *Scorpio*. Believed to be the last survivor of the WC&ICo's canal boats, she is on the Historic Ships Register and is now at the National Boat Museum in Ellesmere Port, Cheshire.

within 'failing, haling, towing, or drawing' boats, barges, lighters, or other vessels with men or horses, or otherwise.'

The rates the controllers of the navigation were empowered to charge were considerable. The provisions of the Act allowed that:

'... in respect of their charges and expenses aforesaid, for all and every such coal, cannel, stone, slate, and other goods, wares, merchandises, and commodities whatsoever, as shall be carried or conveyed in any boat, barges, or other vessel in, upon, to, or from any part of the said River Douglas, alias Asland, between the said River Rible [sic!] *and the said place called Miry Lane End, in the Township of Wigan aforesaid, such rate and duty, rates and duties for tonnage, as the said undertakers, their heirs or assigns, shall think fit, not exceeding two shillings and sixpence for every ton weight of such coal, cannel, stone, slate, and other goods, wares, merchandises, and commodities, and so proportionately for any greater or lesser weight or quantity.'*

In the early 18th century, that was a phenomenally large rate per ton for carriage but the fact that mine owners and other merchants were happy to pay it is a testament to the Navigation's immediate commercial value.

JOHN PARKE & SONS LTD

Today the canal's traffic is made up entirely of leisure craft. Here, a narrowboat passes the former *Way We Were* building on a still autumn morning in October 2015.

In addition to enabling cargo to be carried from Wigan itself, wharfs were constructed at Gathurst to enable coal from the huge and expanding Orrell coalfield to be loaded on to boats – which were, in the early days as Spencer had mentioned, hauled part of the way by gangs of men rather than by horses – and shipped to Preston and beyond.

Surprisingly, Spencer made no mention in his book of its successor, the commercially even more important Leeds to Liverpool Canal, which had already been in use for more than sixty years by the time his book was published, having finally been completed in 1816.

Railways were still more than half a century in the future. While the horse-drawn cart could pull perhaps a few hundredweight or at most two or three tons at a time, the broad horse-drawn barge could carry sixty tons.

The canal system made much of Britain's industrial revolution possible – providing a cheap and effective means of moving large quantities of materials and merchandise around the country, albeit rather slowly.

But, then, it was a time when the pace of life was much more gentle than today and four miles per hour for a laden sixty-ton barge still represented a quicker means of bulk transportation than whatever the total time would have been for the equivalent number of cart journeys.

The canal was built to carry coal, iron, textiles, raw cotton and wool, grain and a hundred other commodities.

left: A horse-drawn barge making its way along the canal near Gathurst in the late 1890s. This view was published as a tinted postcard around 1904.

below left: From almost the same viewpoint, photographed more than a century after the postcard was published, the canal seems just as tranquil, except for the incessant noise of traffic passing over on the M6 motorway.

below: One of the wooden rollers which eased the tow-rope around bridge piers in the days of horse-drawn barges shows the effects of many years of wear. Many of these – with their wear showing their history – were replaced when the area around Wigan Pier was renovated in the 1980s.

Along its banks were built a thousand factories, using its water for their production processes as well as transportation.

Today the canal itself is used for pleasure craft and a significant number of the industrial complexes along the towpath have themselves over the years been turned into major tourist attractions.

The original route of the canal was rather different from the waterway which survives today. Wigan, surprisingly, was well away from the original plans but the town was already served by the Douglas Navigation and there was a measure of competition in the planned route for the

new waterway – the name of which was originally intended to be the Lancashire & Yorkshire Canal.

It required intense lobbying by local mine owners and members of Parliament to persuade the builders to change their route to bring the canal through Wigan. They had the ultimate weapon in their campaign, however, suggesting that if the canal by-passed Wigan, they themselves would dig a cut from the Douglas Navigation all the way towards Liverpool.

As would quickly become apparent, it was in the transportation of Wigan coal to the factories and docks of Liverpool that the canal's real potential for profit lay.

above: Two pleasure craft making their way up the Wigan flight towards Top Lock in the late 1970s.

It is interesting to consider just how different things might have been had they failed to bring about that change of heart – Wigan as a town might not have developed very differently – the mine-owners alternative plans would still have ensured that they were able to meet the ready and growing demand for their coal – but Wigan Pier would never have entered into the folklore of the nation.

below right: As Liverpool Docks developed in the 18th and 19th centuries, becoming the major centre for the importation of raw cotton, mills built along the Leeds & Liverpool Canal had an easy and cost-effective supply route for their raw materials. Liverpool had the same easy access to coal from the Wigan coalfields.

top left: The coal barge *Viktoria* was built in 1934 by W. J. Yarwood & Sons of Northwich. She was a 'dumb' boat with no power of her own, often being propelled by the motor boat *Black Prince*. She is seen here moored by the redeveloped towpath of the Leeds & Liverpool Canal off Swan Meadow Road, just a few yards from the site of James Mayor's Boatyard. She carried grain from Liverpool to Ainscough's Mill at Burscough. *Viktoria* is currently under restoration at Crooke.

left: *Tiger* was one of a fleet of 'fly-boats' operated by the Leeds & Liverpool Canal Company. There would be two men on the boat and a third on the towpath with the horse. The boatman himself – seen here seated on the tarpaulin-covered cargo – was sometimes accompanied by his wife. Indeed, an entire family living and working on a boat was not uncommon. The crewman or crewmen would sleep in the bows of the boat, while the boatman and his family lived at the stern. They all ate together at the stern at meal times.

Despite the fact that Liverpool's docklands were described in the 18th century as the finest complete dock system in the world, the original plans for the canal – the building of which started simultaneously from both Leeds and Liverpool – did not offer any access at all. Indeed, it was well after completion that locks were built joining canal and docks and giving access from the Mersey to what was at the time one of the busiest waterways in the world.

When those locks were completed in 1848, full size 'wide boats' could sail direct from Birkenhead on the other side of the Mersey, straight through to Wigan.

They could also navigate the branches from Rufford to Tarleton, and from Wigan to Leigh. The Rufford to Tarleton

Two views taken in the late 1960s from the terminal grain warehouse, looking down towards the site of Wigan Pier, show the canal almost abandoned, the Wigan Basin filled with sunken boats. Here lie the remains of at least ten dumb boats, including *Plato*, *Cleo*, *Bruno* and *Apollo*. All were part of the fleet of John Parkes & Sons Ltd, canal carriers of Syren Street in Liverpool, who had been a major force on the canal from the early 1900s until 1962. British Waterways took over the traffic that year, with the transportation of coal from Wigan to Liverpool effectively ceasing in 1964.

spur gave access to the Douglas Navigation until that ceased operation, and to the Ribble Estuary and Preston – which then had its own docks – and to the sea.

The Wigan to Leigh spur – which ran through large parts of the coalfield – gave access to the Bridgewater Canal and to the huge network of canals in the Midlands, and eventually also opened up a route to the Manchester Ship Canal.

The opening of the western section of the Leeds & Liverpool Canal hugely expanded the market for Wigan coal. It made possible low cost and reliable bulk transportation on a massive scale.

The standard canal barge had a carrying capacity of sixty tons – several times that of the 30 foot long and 6 foot wide Douglas boats. They were easier to operate, required fewer crew and thus reduced the cost per ton of moving coal quite considerably.

Twenty-four miles from Liverpool Docks, the first of several branches lead off northwards towards Rufford. The branch gave access to the River Douglas and the canal's predecessor the Douglas Navigation, and to the Ribble and Preston which, of course, then had its own docks.

Wigan marked the end of the first stage of building – the canal reached there in 1779 and work stopped. For fifteen years this was the 'end of the cut', until work was restarted in 1794.

above left: The stone-built terminal grain warehouse at Wigan marked the end of the first stage of building. The stretch of canal from Liverpool to Wigan opened to traffic in 1779.

above: The stone warehouses at the Wigan end date from the late 18th century, the brick buildings beyond being added in the 19th. When the Wigan Pier Heritage Centre project was completed, the brick building became the shop and education centre. This photograph was taken in 1985 as renovation neared completion.

It was shortage of cash rather than engineering problems which brought work on the canal to a halt at Wigan and at Gargrave in Yorkshire. The original Leeds to Gargrave section had, strangely, been built to different specifications than the Liverpool to Wigan stretch.

While the canal from Wigan to Liverpool had standard 72 foot long locks able to accommodate two narrow boats side by side, work had started from the Leeds end on locks only 60 feet long. Thus the canal introduced the 'short boat' – the same width as the standard canal barge used throughout the country but 11 feet shorter.

That design decision was partly responsible for the fact that the canal never really assumed the role of major importance within the national waterways network which it might have done.

While short boats could move through the entire canal system, the longer Midlands boats could not be accommodated in the Pennine locks.

Irrespective of the size of the boats, however, canal transportation was less than one third of the cost of moving an equivalent tonnage by road, that saving when passed on having a significant effect on raw material prices. And despite what we think of today as the leisurely pace of movement on the canal, it was actually a lot faster – many roads in the late 18th century were, after all, pretty poor.

'Bantam' tugs were originally designed to power river dredgers but were modified to work on canals. *Bantam 61* (top), photographed in the early 1960s near Wigan, was built in 1957 for British Transport Waterways, forerunners of the British Waterways Board, just after the nationalisation of the canals. *Bantam XXV* (above) was built in 1952 for the Docks & Inland Waterways Executive and based at the Liverpool Docks end of the canal. Despite being known as 'tugs', they actually pushed dumb boats. More than ninety 'Bantams' were constructed.

The normal speed for a boat travelling through the canal would be no more than 3mph, requiring about thirteen hours to reach the Mersey including the time taken to negotiate the locks.

The limiting factor was, of course, the movement of boats through those locks but as there were only nine locks between Wigan and Liverpool, and eleven from Wigan to Tarleton, movement along that stretch of the canal was relatively quick and straightforward. Between four and five hours of that journey time was spent just getting a barge through those locks.

Moving east from Wigan, however, was a much slower business. Climbing up into the hills, the first two miles have twenty-three locks involving the best part of a days' hard work before reaching Top Lock high above the town. Hardly surprising, then, that there was a pub awaiting the exhausted boatmen.

The whole nature of the canal changes from the foot of these locks – relatively flat and easy sailing becomes just a memory as the canal starts the long ascent up through the Pennine Hills. The bargees would have been exhausted by the time they reached the Pennine summit – operating the sluices and opening and closing lock gates still requires a lot of effort today.

To achieve this monumental feat of engineering, however, the designers of the canal had to harness one vital resource in huge quantities. Without water, the system cannot operate and every boat movement through a lock uses around 250,000 litres of water. Rivers were re-routed, huge storage lagoons created and networks of pipes laid to ensure that locks did not run dry. The key to the successful operation of the system, however, ultimately depended on the discipline of the lock-keepers and the boatmen. A sluice or lock gate left open could cause millions of litres of water to go to waste.

left: The route of the canal ran on raised embankments over several of the flashes which had been created by mining subsidence around Wigan and Leigh. Here two coal barges make their way along the cut in the 1950s between Pearson's Flash and Scotsman's Flash, a view obscured today by undergrowth.

below: A small metal plaque records the completion of the final stretch of the canal between Wigan and Gargrave in 1816.

Through Blackburn – and under such delightfully named bridges as 'Paradise' and 'Sour Milk Hall' – the waterway heads towards Burnley and the famous 'Burnley Mile', with the canal carried high above the town on a raised embankment, said to give the finest views of any industrial town in Britain.

The route was originally intended to run much further north, missing Burnley but passing instead close to Padiham. The Shuttleworths of Gawthorpe Hall in Padiham protested in vain against the change of route – required for engineering reasons. Had the original route been followed, Mr Shuttleworth knew the profitability of his collieries, like those in Wigan, would have been significantly enhanced. The Wigan mine-owners were much luckier in the end.

below left: The magazine *The Engineer*, in its issue for 26th April 1895, illustrated a new arrival on the canal when steam dredgers were introduced. They were designed and built for the Leeds & Liverpool Canal Company by Messrs. Cockburn, Philips & Montgomery. *No. 8 Dredger*, seen here, was based at Wigan. Officially known as a 'dredging crane and grab', these steam-powered vessels were then a relatively recent innovation.

Through Nelson – like Blackburn and Burnley built on the cotton industry – and Barrowford, the canal enters Yorkshire and arrives at Gargrave, the terminus of the original section built from Leeds. When work at the Liverpool end reached Wigan, the Yorkshire cut had progressed just over forty miles from Leeds. The fifty mile stretch in between was not completed until 1816.

On the canal today, it is all pleasure craft. The collieries of Wigan which kept a constant stream of barges and 'butty boats', or dumb boats, plying to and fro from Liverpool are all closed. Those factories and mills which are still trading by the towpath now largely use road transport to bring in their materials and take away their merchandise.

The cut remains, though, a testament to the skill and perseverance of 18th century merchants, mine and mill owners, and engineers – and along its banks are many of today's most popular tourist attractions – the heritage museums themselves which tell the story of the 'cut above the rest'.

Just when boat trips along the canal were first advertised as commencing at 'Wigan Pier' is uncertain but the name was certainly in common usage by the 1920s – the most famous postcard, of the steam barge SS *Thomas* loading passengers before departing from Wigan Pier, shows the curved rails of the coal tippler still in place and they were dismantled in 1929.

right: Pleasure craft tied up opposite Trencherfield Mill in the late 1980s.

Boat trips along the canal from Wigan – usually heading west and sometimes going as far as Liverpool – had certainly been in operation since the early years of the 19th century but they invariably were advertised as leaving from Wigan Basin.

From Liverpool, at *'the height of the season'*, seven sailings a day to *'fashionable resorts'* – Southport and Crosby – were augmented by daily sailings to Manchester and Wigan.

Thomas Whitehouse, in his manuscript *History of Wigan* dating from 1820 and illustrated with his own watercolours, noted that passenger sailings to and from Wigan were already commonplace just four years after the canal had finally been completed, having seen an announcement by *'J. Brinson, Agent Office, Canal Wharfe, Wigan'* advertising that:

top: *Severn*, seen here moored under a bridge at Red Rock in the early 1970s, was built by Isaac Pimblott and Sons of Northwich in 1936 for Canal Transport Limited, a major carrier on the Leeds & Liverpool Canal. Their operations were taken over by British Waterways in 1962.

above: A quayside winch and part of the restored towpath, near Seven Stars Bridge, Wigan.

> *'Packet Boats leave in Summer from Wigan Basin every morning at half past eleven, and arrive in Liverpool at eight in the evening. To Manchester every afternoon at half past two and arrive at eight in the evening. During the winter months the Packet departs at eight in the morning and arrives at Liverpool at five in the afternoon. Another Packet leaves Wigan each morning at six and arrives at Manchester at half past eleven o'clock.'*

By 1827, an additional seasonal service to Southport was available, on boats with *'very superior accommodation'* and passengers being met by carriages at Scarisbrick. These were, of course, horse-drawn boats – much safer as the advertisement pointed out, with no chance of *'the frequent accidents attendant on Steam Boats'*.

By the late 18th century, a lengthy rule-book had been drawn up which governed every craft using the canal, with charges and penalties very clearly defined, and woe-betide any boatman who disregarded them. That the 1774 rule-book went into considerable detail about passenger transport charges on the company's own boats suggests that this was a significant aspect of their business plan:

'Every person passing in any boat between Wigan and Liverpool, or any other part of the line, shall pay for every two miles or under, one half-penny; each passenger to be allowed fourteen pounds weight of luggage; and in case any boatman shall neglect to give a just account of the number of passengers he shall at any time carry on his boat, with

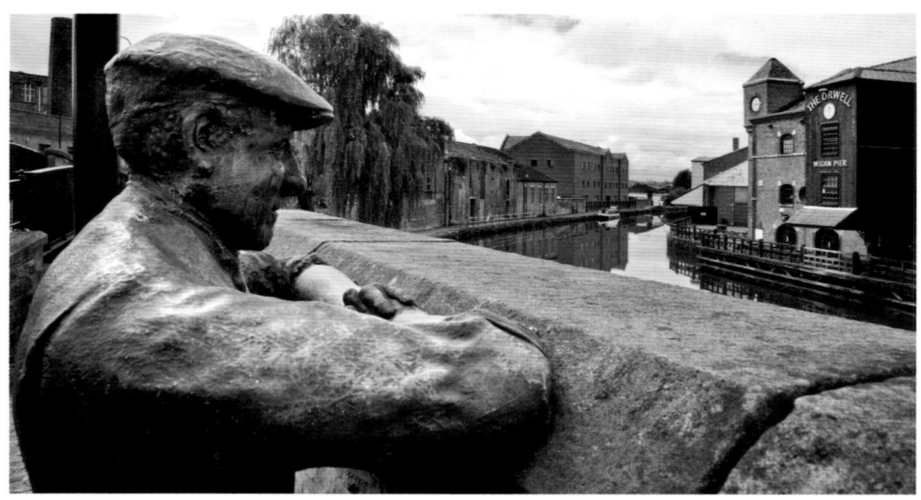

above: The bargee looks out across Wigan Basin from the towpath over Pottery Road Bridge. The replica of Bankes's Pier – now known as Wigan Pier – is by the moored narrowboat in the distance.

right: A heavily laden coal barge makes its way up past the Top Lock Inn, probably in the early 1960s.

the distance each passenger shall have passed, he shall forfeit the sum of ten shillings.'

That must have posed quite a challenger for the boatmen, many of whom were hardly either literate or numerate. Keeping such precise records – and available for inspection at any time during a journey – could not have been easy and in the late 18th century, a ten shilling fine represented a considerable sum of money, probably roughly equivalent to a week's wages. Those rules – especially the '*fourteen pounds weight*' baggage allowance – do conjure up images of some present-day budget

above left: The crew of a coal barge – *en route* from Wigan to Liverpool – pose for the camera in the 1930s.

top: Bridge 69 carries the date of the canal's completion.

above: The milepost at Bridge 69 records the distance to Liverpool.

left: A houseboat undergoing restoration in the dry dock at Wigan Boatyard, the site of the former Mayor's yard.

airlines and presumably required the boatmen to have a set of scales on board to check each piece of luggage.

But it was the transportation of coal which was, and remained, the main lifeblood of the waterway for the next century and a half, with coal loading wharfs and staithes at strategic points along the entire route through the Wigan area. Despite being slow when compared with the growing network of railways, transportation costs per ton were significantly lower by water, and as long as the coal reached its destination at the required time, it didn't really matter to the end-user how long it had taken to get there.

But eventually the coal mines all closed and the small coal-fired power stations they once supplied were taken off-line, leaving the canal without a purpose – except for pleasure craft and fishermen.

The decades of decay which followed would have been a sad end for such a pioneering engineering achievement, and the gradual restoration of the towpaths, the surrounding urban landscape and the waterway itself was a lengthy but eminently worthwhile endeavour. *The Way We Were* enjoyed two decades of success before closing in 2007 but, around Wigan Pier today, another new phase is just beginning.

opposite page: Canal houseboats tied up for the winter at Red Rock, photographed into the fading afternoon sun.

below: Deserted walkways where once there were thronging crowds of visitors – a view along the canal taken just after *The Way We Were* finally closed its doors in 2007.

PATENT
& ROSS

VICTORIAN AND EDWARDIAN WIGAN

THE WIGAN OF THE LATE 19TH CENTURY which gave birth to the Wigan Pier joke was a town dominated by the three great industries of coal, iron and cotton – labour-intensive enterprises which depended on a large and lowly-paid workforce, the efforts of whom made the industrial barons very rich.

At its heart, however, Wigan was still in part a medieval town – narrow lanes and weinds which still retained medieval timber-framed houses could be found just off the main thoroughfares. Indeed, town planning policy in the second half of the 19th century had dictated that new buildings in Standishgate, Wallgate and elsewhere, should be fronted with half-timbered facades to enhance the character of a town which could, after all, trace its history as a commercial centre back to charters in the middle of the 13th century – 1246 to be precise.

But a significant legacy of the town's long history was the poor condition of a large percentage of the housing

opposite: James Nasmyth's original idea for a steam hammer was patented in 1842. A much modified version, patented by William Rigby in 1854, played an important role in the industrial development of Wigan. This 1862 Rigby-design hammer by Glen & Ross of Glasgow, stands outside Trencherfield Mill. By 1889, there were many of these hammers in use in Wigan – the example illustrated came from William Parks & Company's Clarington Forge, while the Pagefield Forge Company had three, '*two of them being fifty hundredweight, and one of four tons.*'

left: 19th century cast-iron railings behind buildings on Wallgate blend harmoniously with the restored Gothic exterior of Wigan's 14th century parish church. Inside, built into a window ledge, a fragment of a Roman altar is a legacy of the Roman settlement of Coccium which once occupied the site.

above: A cigarette card depicting the borough coat of arms, issued c.1902.

above right: Wigan Market Place as it looked c.1800.

right and below: A century later, the Market Place with its half-timbered buildings had been re-invented in Victorian mock-Tudor style to give the town centre the traditional appearance which largely survives today. These two postcards were published around 1904-06. That policy of mock-timbering the fronts of buildings continued throughout the 20th century as well. The setting sun behind the buildings in the middle postcard is an odd piece of Edwardian artistic licence as the shadows cast by the foreground figures makes it clear the sun was behind the camera at the time the photograph was taken.

left: Girls pose by their looms for an Edwardian postcard photographer at John Ryland's huge Gidlow Mill. Originally known as the Gidlow Works, the mill complex had opened in 1868, having been built and equipped at a total cost of £140,968 15s 0d.

stock, much of which had long outlived its usefulness and was particularly ill-matched to the needs and pressures of a rapidly growing population seeking work in the many mills, collieries and engineering works. Thus, living conditions for the majority of the town's workforce were in many cases – largely as a result of overcrowding – much worse than they had been a century earlier. As a result of the enormous growth in both mining and cotton production in the second half of the 19th century, the town's population was growing faster than the infrastructure could keep up with. By the end of the century, overcrowding was widespread, with all the problems of poor sanitation and poor health.

Working in a damp cotton mill was unhealthy enough, without having to return after work to homes which offered few, if any, creature comforts. And yet, Victorian Wigan prided itself in the advances it claimed to have made in its water supply and in public health.

In an account of the major Lancashire towns originally published in 1889 by The Historical Publishing Company – reprinted in 1990 by Landy Publishing as *Wigan a Century Ago* – the writer described Wigan as:

> '... *being governed by a singularly enlightened and progressive corporation, which does its utmost to forward the best interests of the borough. So far back as 1761 Wigan obtained an Act of Parliament by which it produced an*

below: Amongst the improvements which were made to roads in Lancashire in the first half of the 19th century, elaborate, cast-iron mileposts were installed along the major trunk routes. This one was cast at Haigh Foundry in 1837, one of the town's major ironworks at the time.

excellent water supply, and it was one of the first towns to be lighted by gas, an Act having been procured and a company formed in 1823.'

The description of the town continued in similar vein, noting that:

'... special attention has been directed by the powers that be to the sanitary condition of the town, an all-important matter in a town like Wigan.'

He does not, however, give any idea of just how widespread the good sanitation, the excellent water supply, or the wide and well-paved roads actually were. The truth was such Victorian luxuries did not extend to many of the poorer parts of the town at all. For most people, access to fresh water was a single communal hand-pump in a shared yard – a supply inside the house was a luxury indeed.

Sanitary conditions in Wigan were actually no worse than in most other towns. A sewerage system had

been established in and around the town centre in the 1850s but its raw effluent was discharged into the River Douglas – so better sanitation for some actually led to a poorer living environment for those who lived anywhere near the river.

The government had set up a Royal Sanitary Commission in 1868 to establish the current state of affairs within English towns and cities – and seek ways of unifying all the separate Acts of Parliament which had facilitated local sewage systems into a single national set of minimum standards.

One of the commissioners appointed was Wigan-born Francis Sharp Powell – later Baronet – who would, from 1885 until 1910, serve as the town's Member of Parliament.

Democracy, even in the closing years of the 19th century, was a very limited privilege. Powell, the Conservative candidate, was returned to Parliament having polled just 3,371 votes, while his Liberal opponent polled 2,870. That, however, represents an 85% turnout from the 7,000 registered electors of the day – 7,000 people with the right to vote out of a population in the borough of somewhere around 50,000. Twenty years earlier, there had been fewer than 4,500 electors out of a population just short of 40,000.

Rightly celebrated was Wigan's premier open green space, Mesnes Park – referred to in the text by the more archaic name of '*Meynes Park*' – which opened in 1878, one of many open spaces to be created in the hearts of industrial towns at the time.

Described as the '*lungs of the town*', it was regularly enjoyed at dinner times by the workers at nearby John Ryland's Gidlow Mills, the empty and derelict remains of which today cast an unfortunate shadow over the recently restored park.

In a town parts of which had more than its fair share of high density back-to-back terraced housing, this open green space with its pavilion and bandstand proved immediately popular with Wiganers and has been enjoyed by the community ever since. A major restoration project in recent years has returned it to its Victorian glory.

opposite, from top: a view of the Mesnes Park Pavilion taken in the 1890s and published as a postcard c.1904; A 1903 postcard showing the 1878 cast-iron Coalbrookdale fountain in front of the pavilion. An exact replica of the fountain was sited in the original location in 2014 – the original having been removed in 1921; John Ryland's Gidlow Mills, which overlooked the park, from a postcard c.1910; a panoramic view, late 1990s.

below: The 1910 statue of Wigan-born Sir Francis Sharp Powell in Mesnes Park. Locals rubbing his shoe for good luck wore it into holes. Recently it has been restored and cleaned.

left: Photographed around 1890, this is believed to be one of the workshops at Walker Brothers' Pagefield Forge Company adjacent to their Pagefield Ironworks. Much of the machinery in the plant was steam driven, the boilers being heated by waste heat from the blast furnaces.

below: Swinley Road in 1905, an avenue of elegant housing for the wealthy of the town, looked across to St. Michael's Church, designed in 1875 by George Edmund Street and completed in 1878.

opposite page: Wigan's foundries had an international reputation for quality and their steam engines were exported across the world. Bursledon Brickworks in Hampshire has the only surviving operational single cylinder steam engine by John Wood & Co., built c.1885 at their Water Heyes Foundry.

inset: Swing bridges and cast-iron columns, for Liverpool's Albert Dock were manufactured at Haigh Foundry and shipped part of the way to the site by canal boat from Wigan Basin.

Given that Sir Francis Sharp Powell had been instrumental, nationally, in raising the profile of public health and sanitation, it is fitting that the town erected a statue to him in the centre of Mesnes Park.

Over the years, so many people touched his shoe as they passed – said to be for good luck – that a hole was worn into the bronze. Restored in 2013, the statue is now a pristine bronze colour once again, stripped of the patina of age.

top: A 1904 view of the blast furnaces at the Kirkless ironworks of the Wigan Coal & Iron Company, formed in 1865 by the amalgamation of the collieries owned by the Earl of Crawford and Balcarres, the ironworks and collieries of the Kirkless Hall Company, the Broomfield Colliery Company and the Standish & Shevington Coal and Cannel Company. By 1890, the company had a workforce of more than 10,000, and owned thirty-two steam locomotives and 5,500 coal wagons.

right & below: The Semet Solvay electric ovens at Kirkless produced the vast amounts of coke needed to keep the blast furnaces operating. The American Semet-Solvay process also recovered other minerals from the coal usually lost during coking. These two c.1905 images come from a series of views by local photographer James Millard. The installation of the forty-four electric ovens was of sufficient importance to warrant the publication of a highly detailed four-page article in May that year in the journal *The Electrical Review*.

top: The image of the town most commonly presented by Wigan's postcard manufacturers was far removed from the industrial scenes. It showed a much more picturesque aspect, and included this view of the Marylebone area on Wigan Lane. This postcard dates from c.1910.

middle: The pupils of Notre Dame Convent on Standishgate wait to greet King George V during his visit to the town on 10th July 1913. At the time this photograph was taken, 9-year old George Formby Junior was one of the children in the school's primary department so he may even be one of the boys in the front row. Three days before this picture was taken, his father had taken part in a Royal Command Performance at Knowsley Hall, where the King and Queen were staying as guests of Lord Derby.

bottom: Walker Brothers built the huge fans which ventilated many of Britain's coal mines – some able to pump a million cubic feet of air a minute down into deep mines. This one dates from the early 20th century.

right: The Coach & Horses at No. 1 Hallgate was a throwback to Wigan's medieval past, one of the oldest coaching inns in the town dating back to the 16th century. Around the time this photograph was taken, c.1889 and probably by John Cooper, the landlord was Thomas Holcroft, who also ran the Griffin in Standishgate. It was demolished a few years after this picture was taken.

below: Jolley's Celebrated Old Dog Music Hall and Concert Rooms was attached to the inn of the same name in Cooper's Row, next to the Alexandra. The building was demolished in the 1970s.

A survey of Wigan's many manufacturing enterprises in the late 19th century makes remarkable reading. This was a town at the forefront of heavy engineering and industrial manufacturing.

The Wigan Coal & Iron Company, Pagefield Ironworks, Haigh Foundry, John Wood & Co., the Roburite Explosives Company at nearby Gathurst and many others, exported to just about every corner of the world. In the 1880s, the Wigan Coal & Iron Company advertised that its output exceeded 125,000 tons of iron a year.

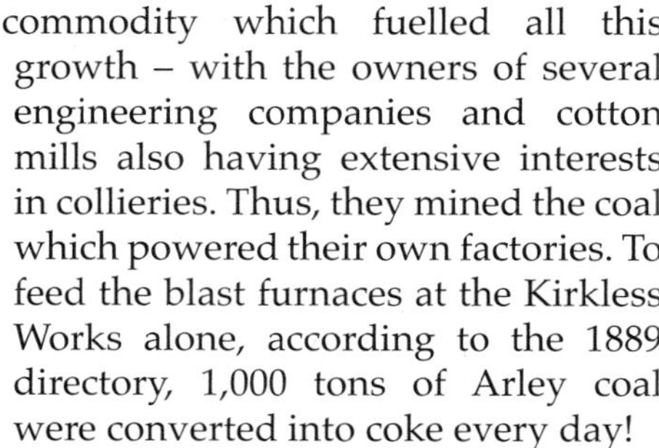

Coal was the commodity which fuelled all this growth – with the owners of several engineering companies and cotton mills also having extensive interests in collieries. Thus, they mined the coal which powered their own factories. To feed the blast furnaces at the Kirkless Works alone, according to the 1889 directory, 1,000 tons of Arley coal were converted into coke every day!

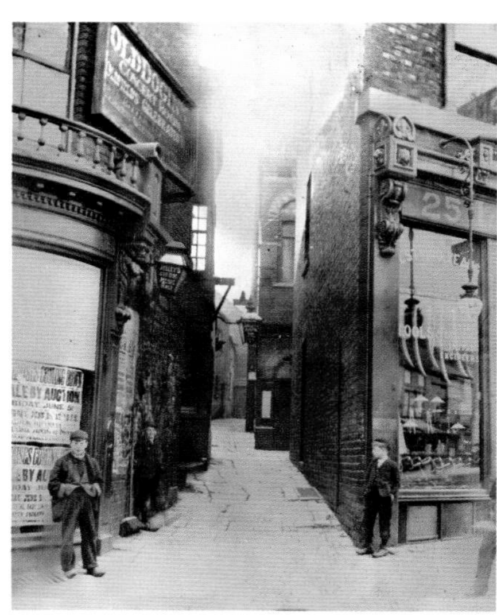

This meant that a huge quantity of coal was being moved around the area every day, requiring, as well as the Leeds & Liverpool Canal – the key transport route in and out of the town – a network of waggonways which were used to move coal around the immediate area.

Waggonways played a pivotal role both in the success of Wigan's industries and also, ironically, in the creation of the mythical Wigan Pier which led to the joke – but more of that later.

The establishment of the main line railway networks would take much of the transport off the canals, with the opening of the Wigan Junction Railway in 1832, the North Union Railway in 1838 – both eventually becoming part of the London & North Western Railway in 1846 – and the Lancashire & Yorkshire Railway in 1848. Coal, however, would continue to be shipped to Westwood Power Station by canal into the 1970s.

While mills, ironworks and factories in the first half of the 19th century were usually built with local access to the canal, the second half of the century saw demand for industrial land alongside the burgeoning railway network grow and hugely increase in value.

Away from the mills and factories, the spiritual and social needs of the population were met by numerous churches of every denomination, public houses and music halls.

Wigan's first purpose-built music hall – a proper theatre as opposed to rowdier establishments in pubs, as was the widespread Victorian practice – was the Alexandra on Cooper's Row, which opened its doors on 6th April 1874.

The *Wigan Observer* believed it to be a significant development for the town, describing the interior in great detail:

above: Music Hall star Vesta Tilley appeared at the Alexandra Music Hall in 1891, one of many leading entertainers to appear in the theatre. This portrait of her was taken a few years later and published as a postcard by Brown, Barnes & Bell, a national chain of studios, the Wigan branch of which had opened at 30 Standishgate in 1881.

left: The Alexandra Music Hall was opposite the pub now known as the John Bull Chophouse, which has stood in The Weind since the 16th century. The paved roadway which separates the pub from the site of the theatre is one of the oldest paved streets in Wigan.

right: For more than a century, Wigan's 1877 Market Hall served the town well, although for much of its 20th century life it looked nothing like this – the elegant canopied arcades which surrounded it having been replaced by shops. It was demolished in 1989.

above: James Millard standing outside the 1881 wooden studio he had built opposite the Market Hall. It stood on the site later occupied by the Queen's Hall. The Millards were portrait photographers in the town for more than fifty years. Louisa Millard had opened a studio in Hope Street in 1865, her brother James opening his studio in Millgate in 1872 – the year Lucy married and became Lucy Mawson. James also ran a second studio at Scholes Bridge from 1875 until 1898.

'On entering the building the first thing to attract attention will no doubt be the ingenious way in which the space, which on the ground floor seems very small, has been utilised for the accommodation of the public; and it will scarcely be credited that room is provided for nearly 1000 persons. This is done however by the house being divided into three parts: a commodious pit, eleven feet above that a balcony; and eight feet higher a gallery, the latter being fourteen feet from the ceiling. The proscenium is seventeen feet wide in the clear and twenty five feet high; and the manner in which it is decorated is one of the most attractive features of the hall. The style of decoration is Italian; a blue ground is brought out in elegant designs of crimson, white, gold and green, and the proscenium is surmounted with the national coat of arms.'

The theatre later became the Empire Palace Music Hall. Among the stars who performed on its stage in 1898 was George Formby Snr, who would later play a pivotal role in the story of Wigan Pier and the propagation of the joke.

Between the Alexandra and Market Place, on the corner site, was the long-established Jolley's Old Dog Inn and attached music hall, which had itself been given a make-over before re-opening to the public in 1886.

Alehouses were something the Victorian town was not short of, with more than one hundred and fifty listed in the 1869 *Trade Directory* – the first to be published in Wigan – which covered the larger area known as the Wigan Union, together with more than three hundred '*Beer Retailers*' and seven establishments retailing wines and spirits.

Between Market Place and Seven Stars Bridge, there were more than a dozen public houses on Wallgate, nine in Market Place, and fourteen on Standishgate and Wigan Lane between Market Place and Swinley Road. There was but a single Temperance Hotel, run by Thomas Nicholson in Rowbottom Square.

Some of the town's more enterprising publicans realised the potential of the new medium of photography in the 1860s. Anticipating that in a town like Wigan, photography alone would not provide an adequate income, makeshift studios were opened in several inns and public houses from the early 1860s – Thomas Dugdale, landlord of the Green Man Inn in Standishgate, started advertising his services as a photographer as early as 1863. He would later move from the Green Man to an address in Upholland, to be replaced as landlord and studio proprietor by John Cooper, formerly a beer retailer, who would become perhaps the best known Victorian recorder of the sights of Wigan. It is through Cooper's lens that we see what the town looked like before the wholesale redevelopment in the last quarter of the 19th century.

above: Wigan's own Police Force existed from 1836 until merged with the Lancashire Constabulary in April 1969. Five years later it was moved again to become part of Greater Manchester Police.

below: At the time the Market Hall was completed in 1877, a new Market Square was laid out next to it – since lost beneath The Galleries. One account noted that '*On Market Days, which are Tuesdays and Fridays, and especially on the latter, the Square is transformed. In the early morning hours, carts containing produce of all kinds begin to arrive from the surrounding districts, and their goods are quickly removed. The market is celebrated; a splendid collection of produce sold direct from farmers' carts is not a common sight in manufacturing towns.*' This animated postcard dates from around 1905.

Cooper had set up his first studio in Harrogate Street in 1863, moving to the Royal Oak Hotel in Standishgate in 1866, then to the Green Man around 1872, before taking over the Harrogate Inn. In the mid-1890s, he established a photographic business in Poolstock – by which time Dugdale had returned with his cameras to the Green Man.

Others combining two occupations included John Barton, photographer, confectioner and beer seller in Lamberhead Green, Robert Bibby, photographer and confectioner in Water Heyes, and James Platt, photographer and insurance agent in Church Street.

When he opened his first studio in Millgate in 1872, James Millard advertised himself as *'Photographer, Hardware Dealer, Auctioneer, Valuer, Optician and Picture Framer'*.

below: Huge steam engines were once a common sight in Wigan's many cotton mills before electricity took over. The 2,500hp Trencherfield Mill Engine, built by J. & E. Wood at their Victoria Foundry in Bolton in 1908, is the last survivor in the town and now beautifully restored, it is the largest working mill engine in the world. Steam was originally raised using local Wigan coal but it now runs on biofuel.

above: Edwardian Wallgate echoed twice daily to the clattering of clogs as hundreds of women made their way to and from work at the many mills in the area – Eckersley's Swan Meadow Mills, Trencherfield, Pennyhurst, Taylors, and others.

It is remarkable that, from that early heyday of photography, images of the canal and its piers seem to be very rare. On the basis of surviving pictures, photographers appear to have limited themselves to either taking views of public buildings, or making studio portraits of Wiganers. Perhaps the coal piers along the canal were considered to be unworthy subjects for photography.

Late 19th century Wigan was still a market town at heart, despite its growing industrial success. With cotton mills employing thousands of skilled and semi-skilled men, women and children, and ringed by the rich coalfields, unemployment was low but so were wages.

This, then, was the town into which 16 year old James Booth Lawler arrived some time in 1892, to perform in local pubs and music halls as part of a musical duo known as 'The Brothers Glenray'. History seems to have forgotten the name of the boy – reportedly with a beautiful tenor voice – who was the other half of the duo.

When that partnership broke up and James decided to carve out a solo career for himself, he chose the stage name of George Formby. He had already found out that he could make people laugh and his soprano voice was, presumably, getting less reliable as he got older. He would later claim to have been born in Wigan but had, in fact, been born and brought up in abject poverty in Ashton-under-Lyne.

His son, George Formby of banjolele fame was, however, a Wiganer, having been born in his parents' home at 3 Westminster Street – the approximate site of which is now marked with a blue plaque.

Without them both, father and son, Wigan's enduring fame throughout the world might never have come about.

below: As the 19th century drew to a close, another Wigan institution was born. In 1898, the town's most famous confection was created – Uncle Joe's Mint Balls – establishing a business which is still owned by the Santus family today.

WIGAN'S COALFIELDS

BRITAIN'S APPETITE FOR COAL in the second half of the 19th century was almost insatiable. Railway networks were expanding, the Royal Navy was converting from sail to steam, ever-larger passenger and cargo steamers were being built, and mills and factories were converting from water-power to steam-power to meet ever-growing demands for their produce. Coal produced gas for street and house lighting, and coke fed blast furnaces operating around the clock to manufacture iron and steel.

Meeting those demands made a few people very rich and directly provided back-breaking work for thousands of men and women in the Wigan area alone. Indirectly it also provided a great deal of work for many others – on the railways and canals – moving the coal around the area and further afield across the growing transport networks.

The price paid for that coal, in human hardship and loss of life, was considerable – Wigan's deep mines suffered from firedamp gas, especially at times of high atmospheric pressure, and as colliers were working sometimes several thousand feet below ground and even further from the

opposite page: From the early 1980s until 2013, a colliery winding wheel stood on the frontage of Wigan & Leigh College – an unused spare wheel from a local pit – facing on to Parsons Walk. As a result of development of some of the college buildings, it has since been moved round the corner, sadly to a less prominent position.

above: Sacks of coal were once delivered to almost every household.

left: Two of the terms used to describe coal were 'Black Gold' and 'Black Diamonds', so important was it to Britain's success. Wigan steam coal powered the ships, railways and industrial engines which drove the expansion of the Victorian and Edwardian Empire.

bottom of the pit shaft, attempts at rescue when anything did go wrong were slow and frequently unsuccessful endeavours.

And yet coal defined the town from the early 16th century right up to the last deep mine closure as recently as 1992. That was the huge Bickershaw Colliery, which worked the Parsonage and Golborne seams as well, and when it closed, all that was left were the slag heaps.

In the second half of the 19th century, over 9,000 men were employed as colliers with the Wigan Union – that number swelled considerably when surface workers, both men and women, were taken into account.

In the 1860s, there were nearly fifty different collieries in operation, bringing to the surface more than four million tons of coal every year. As the century grew to a close, the number of collieries had increased considerably, the output had more than doubled and the workforce – above and below ground – had risen steadily towards 20,000.

While the majority of the workers were men, Wigan's famous pit brow lasses – or pit wenches as they were sometimes called – created an added interest in the town's workforce when photography came along.

Most Victorians had never seen women undertake the heavy work which the pit girls carried out daily, and marketing photographs of these sturdy women proved an interesting commercial sideline for the towns first studios

opposite page: Robert Little, one of the first photographers to open a studio in Wigan – in Clarence Yard in 1853 – took many photographs of Wigan's pit brow lasses and published them as *cartes-de-visite*, the small prints which fitted into the Victorian family album. This study was taken c.1865 and is shown here several times actual size. To take a studio photograph in the early days required a long exposure so, as an aid to keeping the subjects still while the picture was being taken, heavy cast iron stands were placed behind them with head clamps to minimise movement, the bases of which can be seen behind the feet of each woman.

left: Photographing underground – especially in mines where there was a risk of gas – was dangerous, so images like this, taken in 1898 are relatively unusual. A large electric lamp, a heavy wooden camera and all the paraphernalia of early photography had to be taken deep below ground. This picture was subsequently published as a tinted postcard by James Starr about six years later.

above: *Carte-de-visite* portraits of pit girls, taken by John Cooper at his Harrogate Street studio, 1865.

below: Tinted Edwardian postcards of pit brow girls were produced in great numbers.

– studios more accustomed to taking portraits of people in their 'Sunday best'.

Arthur Munby, a civil servant from London, was one of many who purchased *cartes-de-visite* of Wigan pit brow lasses. Clearly fascinated by all working women, the Wigan girls were just one of his enthusiasms.

Writing in his diaries – now preserved in the Wren Library at Cambridge – he wrote of his visits to the town and his encounters with local photographers.

In so doing, he touched upon the widely held view that women should not be seen in breeches – some had even suggested that women thus dressed were an affront to their sex and a temptation to men!:

> *'Friday 17 March 1865: Fine sunny morning: afterwards cold and cloudy, with keen east wind. I went out at nine to the photographers: to Dugdale, who has at length taken a group of pit wenches at a colliery near Telure's, towards*

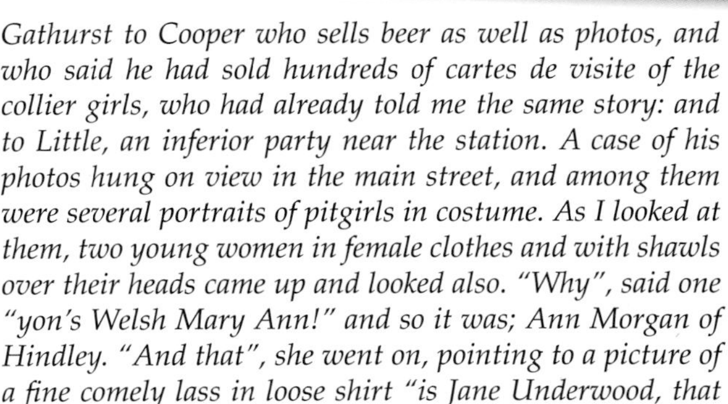

Gathurst to Cooper who sells beer as well as photos, and who said he had sold hundreds of cartes de visite of the collier girls, who had already told me the same story: and to Little, an inferior party near the station. A case of his photos hung on view in the main street, and among them were several portraits of pitgirls in costume. As I looked at them, two young women in female clothes and with shawls over their heads came up and looked also. "Why", said one "yon's Welsh Mary Ann!" and so it was; Ann Morgan of Hindley. "And that", she went on, pointing to a picture of a fine comely lass in loose shirt "is Jane Underwood, that

above: Safety lamps played a major part in improving Victorian mine safety. J.H. Naylor of Wigan was one of the many manufacturers. Two can be seen in the postcard *above left.*

left: At the National Coal Mining Museum for England, a recreation of the back yard of a collier's terraced house c.1900. For many colliers' families, however, having a privy in their own back yard would have seemed a luxury compared with the communal toilets most of them still had to endure.

From Dugdale, Cooper and Little, right through to the years before the First World War, Wigan's pit brow lasses regularly posed for local photographers. These 1904-1910 postcard studies were taken by Thomas Taylor and James Millard.

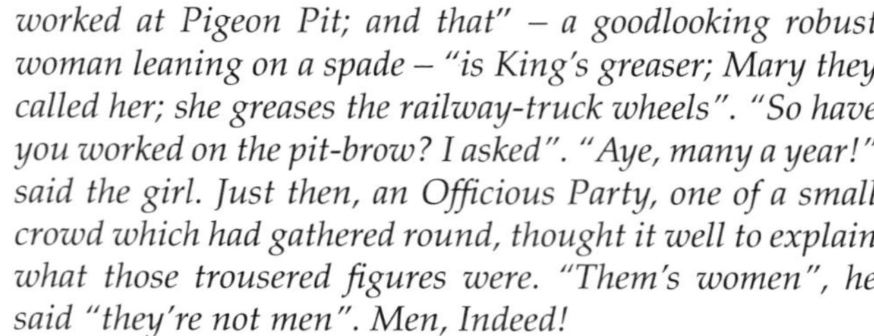

worked at Pigeon Pit; and that" – a goodlooking robust woman leaning on a spade – "is King's greaser; Mary they called her; she greases the railway-truck wheels". "So have you worked on the pit-brow? I asked". "Aye, many a year!" said the girl. Just then, an Officious Party, one of a small crowd which had gathered round, thought it well to explain what those trousered figures were. "Them's women", he said "they're not men". Men, Indeed!

All the four photographers said they sold these photos chiefly to commercial travellers, who buy them as 'curiosities'. "Many strangers passes their remarks upon 'em", said Mrs. Little; "and some considers as it's a shame for women to wear breeches, and some take it for a joke, like". Just so: some are sentimentalists, some sensualists: none rational and serious.'

Despite Munby's low opinion of Robert Little's skills – dismissing him as *'an inferior party near the station'* – he was happy enough to have Little take photographs of him with one of the girls, Ellen Grounds aged 22, who was nearly as tall as he was – and he was a tall man himself. As well as the height comparison, she was also wearing trousers.

The local debate about the modesty or otherwise of women wearing trousers clearly fascinated him and on one earlier occasion in 1863 he had noted in his diary that:

'They told me ... that the Haydock pits are the nearest to St. Helens of all those where this Wigan costume prevails;

SUCKER PIT
NOTICE
F. SPENCER 06
Boss of Sucker Pit, to Collier.—"It's no use thee comin' here wi' a yed like that, tha' mon be bawd so's wi' con let thi' down wi' a Sucker."
(Copyright.) WILL SMITH'S SERIES, Wigan

THE LOSS OF SEVENTY LIVES IN A BURNING MINE AT WIGAN.

The mining industry gave rise to a whole range of humorous postcards from local publisher Will Smith of Wigan Lane. Here, in a scene at the fictitious 'Sucker Pit', the boss is explaining to a miner with a full head of hair that unless he shaves himself bald, there will be no way of attaching the sucker pad on the end of a rope to his head with which to lower him deep down into the workings.

Coal mining also caused great hardship and loss of life. In August 1908, both the *Illustrated London News* and the local newspaper, the *Wigan Observer,* devoted an entire page each to pictures of the Maypole Pit disaster in which seventy-six men lost their lives. This sort of press photography was a relatively new innovation, thanks to improvements in the printing processes used for magazines and newspapers since the beginning of the century. For the first time, photographs could be reproduced on the printed page. When disasters like this could strike at any time, it is no surprise that the colliers developed a suitably black sense of humour at times.

A late Victorian view of an unidentified barge, heavily laden, beneath Crooke Coal Pier. The arrival of the photographer was clearly an unusual event for the village, with many locals turning out to be included in the picture. The first tippler was built here before 1812, at the end of Clark's Tramroad, originally a 4-foot gauge wagonway from the Orrell coalfield to the canal. At least four – successively larger – structures have occupied the site, the last being built in the 1950s. It was the last of the large tipplers in the Wigan area to be dismantled. The waggonway was the first to be steam-hauled.

and so it was. Black Brook is a Rubicon which no pit-wench in 'breeches' may pass. From this pit I could see the canal quay, with its female workers only 200 or 300 yards off; yet those women 'reckoned they'd be ashamed' to dress thus, while these walked about in their trousers with utmost indifference – and, I may add, with no less modesty than the others in their kirtles.'

Long after it had been declared illegal in 1842, some Wigan women even dressed as men so they could still work underground 'on the sly'.

Working on the pit brow was, however, an occupation considered to be much less injurious to health than working in the damp conditions of a cotton mill. Young girls were by no means reluctant to take on this onerous occupation – at least until they got married – swelling the numbers employed in the coalfields considerably.

Underground, life was much harder – Wigan's coalfields suffered regularly from build-ups of gas, so ventilating them and keeping the colliers safe underground was a primary concern for both mine owners and government inspectors.

Sometimes those best efforts were not enough, and explosions deep underground caused havoc and loss of life. The most widely-reported of them was the explosion at the

Maypole Colliery on 18th August 1908, where gas ignited during the regular shot-firing operations which were carried out to blast the coal out of the seams.

In dealing with that explosion, innovations such as gas masks and breathing apparatus were used by the rescue teams who ventured into the workings to search for survivors and recover the dead.

Local companies manufacturing everything from miners' lamps to pit props – and the huge ventilating fans which Walker Brothers exported in large numbers – further considerably swelled the number of people dependent on coal for their livelihoods.

Wigan's coal seams extended more than 2,500 feet below ground – twenty-six clearly defined seams, each with particular characteristics which ensured there was a ready market for the output, from domestic use through to the highly prized 'steam coal' which powered the ships, railways and factories of Victorian Britain. Thus, Wigan coal needed to be dispersed widely across Britain.

The widening and deepening of the River Douglas – the Douglas Navigation – in the 18th century had quickly proved inadequate for the coalfield's growing output, so the cutting of the first section of the Leeds & Liverpool Canal in the 1790s was a pivotal development. Without the canal, transporting ever-increasing quantities of coal would have been a slow and commercially unattractive proposition. The low shipping costs of the canal made an enormous difference – and gave rise to Wigan's first piers.

One of the first to recognise the commercial value of a combination of railway and canal for the transportation of vast quantities of coal was the engineer Robert Dalglish, who had arrived in Wigan in 1804 to take over the role of Superintendent

below: The Mine Rescue team, based at the Lancashire & Cheshire Coal Owners Rescue Station at Howe Bridge, played a key role during several colliery disasters.

bottom: This certificate, which was issued to those who successfully completed the rescue training programme at Howe Bridge, is now displayed in the National Coal Mining Museum for England near Wakefield.

right: *Yorkshire Horse*, the locomotive built at Haigh by Robert Dalglish under licence from John Blenkinsop. The cogged central wheel meshed into a rack on the outside of one of the rails. The locomotive had 8ins diameter cylinders with a 24ins stroke, developed 14hp and had a top speed of 4mph. It could pull a thirty wagon train carrying 90 tons of coal, a total load of around 125 tons.

below & opposite: The 0-6-0ST tank engine *Lindsay* was built in 1887 by and for the Wigan Coal & Iron Company and operated in their Gidlow Washeries. It was restored to full working order and returned to steam in 1987. Many of the WC&ICo.'s locomotives incorporated design features more usually found on main line engines. The Chief Engineer and General Manager at the Kirkless works at the time, Thomas Percy, had worked at the London & North Western Railway's locomotive works at Crewe before joining the Wigan company. *Lindsay* had 16ins cylinders, making it a very powerful small locomotive for its day. It was approved to operate on both the L&NWR and L&YR main lines.

REGISTERED BY THE
No 149
1952
RAILWAY EXECUTIVE
WIGAN

of the Earl of Crawford and Balcarres' Haigh Foundry and Brock Mill Forge.

By 1812, he had become manager of John Clarke's Orrell Colliery and his engineering company – Robert Dalglish & Company – was already establishing a reputation for the construction of innovative and efficient stationary colliery steam engines.

Dalglish immediately recognised the potential value of replacing the horses on Clarke's waggonway with steam traction and sought the rights to manufacture a novel locomotive – designed and patented by John Blenkinsop of Leeds – and operate it on his waggonway.

The locomotive, known as the *Yorkshire Horse* and built at Haigh Foundry, proved an immediate success, hauling

opposite: A group of engineers pose on one of their locomotives at Blundells Pemberton Colliery c.1920. All of the large collieries had their own railway yards; many also built their own locomotives and had engineering workshops to keep their fleets operational.

Billinge, an 0-4-0ST outside cylinder saddle tank engine, was built by Andrew Barclay at Kilmarnock in 1916 and was one of three locomotives which worked at the Leyland Green Pit, part of the Winstanley Collieries complex. This type of locomotive was widely used on colliery railways, and at least two of this design and vintage still survive but sadly *Billinge* is not amongst them.

Orrell, an 0-4-0ST locomotive, was built to work in the coal yards of Blundells' Collieries. While many were purchased from established makers, *Orrell* may well have been constructed by Jonathan Blundell & Son in the colliery's own engineering shop. No precise date for this photograph can be established but it probably dates from c.1890.

below: A scene at Elms Colliery in Whitley during the 1912 miners' strike. Coal picking or scrabbling was considered unusual enough then to attract several local photographers and be printed as postcards but by the time Orwell wrote his account of the town in 1936, it had clearly become an essential way of life for the poor and the unemployed. At Elms, in addition to seams of what was known locally as King Coal – a high quality steam coal – there was a lot of cannel, rich pickings for the scrabblers over the years, and although the pit had closed a year before Orwell's visit, the spoil heaps were still good sources of fuel.

wagons of coal from Clark's John Pit at Orrell to Crooke Pier on the Leeds & Liverpool Canal. It used a rack and cog system to improve traction, a system which is still used in many mountain railways today.

Dalglish built several other locomotives – later abandoning the cog-drive system as this proved an unnecessary aid to traction and replacing that by driving two of the wheels. It has been suggested that one of them later worked the waggonway from Lamb & Moore's colliery to Banke's Pier – the tippler near the Wigan Basin which is today celebrated as Wigan Pier.

Yorkshire Horse was small by the standards of later locomotives – weighing only six tons and developing just 14 horse-power – but it established the enormous commercial value of steam in the movement of large quantities of coal. It burned a little over a hundredweight of coal per hour – effectively a free fuel as far as colliery owners were concerned – and proved extremely reliable. Its working life was short, however, as more and more powerful locomotives were introduced.

Locomotives were much faster than horses and faster than the steam-powered winch systems which had initially replaced those horses. And, of course, they could move much more coal at a time than either.

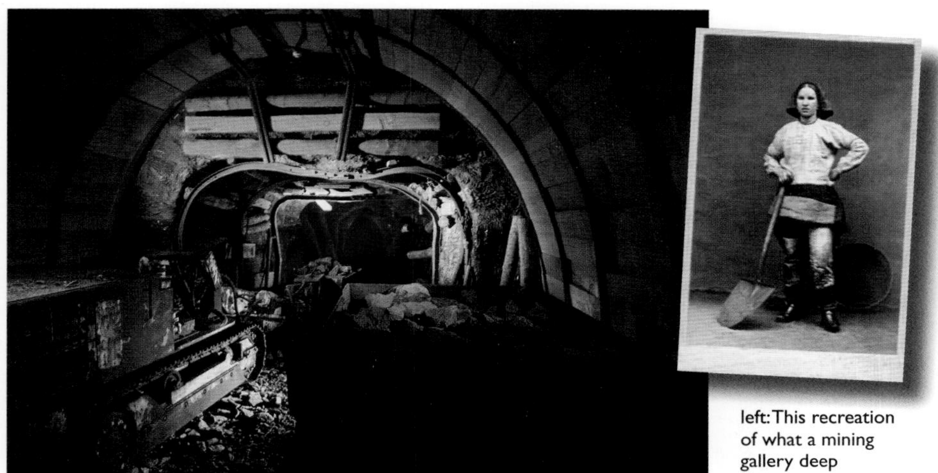

left: This recreation of what a mining gallery deep underground looked like gives a real sense of the constant geological pressures which more than 2,000 feet of rock could bring to bear on the roof supports over the roadways and the workings. When many pits closed, it was simply uneconomic to return the larger pieces of equipment to the surface. They are still down there.

above: A pit lass photographed in the studio of John Cooper around 1865. Women continued to work in Wigan's pityards for a further century, the numbers declining before the Second World War but then actually rising during the war and into the 1950s. Women ceased to be employed in the colliery yards in the late 1960s.

Just when the name of Crooke Pier was attached to the coal staithe is uncertain – in the 19th century it was variously referred to as the Crooke Tip or Crooke Tippler. The same uncertainty hangs over a number of the other 'piers' on the canal and there is a strong suggestion that some of them actually only became commonly known as 'piers' once the idea of Wigan Pier had gained widespread currency.

Three main features characterised the vast Wigan coalfields – firstly there was an awful lot of coal. Between the surface and a depth of around 2,000 feet, there were many seams, offering more than eighty feet of coal. Secondly, Wigan lies on five geological fault lines and rock movement over the millennia means that none of those seams is continuous. Some rise almost to the surface – profitable drift mines capitalised on these seams – while others, deep below ground, suddenly disappear, only to reappear many feet below.

Thirdly, and most importantly for the colliery owners of Wigan, much of the coal was of premium quality, yielding a high heat output and leaving little residue in the way of clinker or ash. The best produced high quality steam coal for transport and industry; others yielded coking coal, ideal for gas generation, and for iron and steel smelting.

Most celebrated of Wigan's coal was 'cannel' or 'candle' coal, which had a very high calorific value and was so combustible that it could be lit directly from a match. It was a very fine and evenly textured coal – a quality which local sculptors quickly discovered. They used it to make carved busts and plaques of local colliery owners, and even turned it on lathes to create plates and serving dishes. It could be polished to a high gloss and despite its origins, was remarkably clean to handle.

Tradition has it that after a particular dinner at Haigh Hall, with part of the meal eaten off cannel coal platters, they were then used to stoke the fire!

The characteristics of cannel coal had been known for centuries. In his book *A Tour Through the Whole Island of Great Britain*, Daniel Defoe – of *Robinson Crusoe* fame – was one of the first to write about its qualities, as early as 1725:

> *'In the neighbourhood of this town is found that kind of coal they call Canell or Candle Coal, which, though they are found here in great plenty, and are very cheap, are yet very singular; for there are none such to be seen in Britain, or perhaps in the world besides. They so soon take fire, that, by putting a lighted candle to them, they are presently in a flame, and yet hold fire for so long as any coals whatever, and more or less, as they are placed in the grate or hearth, whether flat or edged, whether right up and down, and polar, or level and horizontal.*
>
> *They are smooth and slick when the pieces part from one another, and will polish like alabaster; then a lady may take them up in a cambric handkerchief and they will not soil it, though they are as black as the deepest jet. They are the most pleasant, agreeable fuel that can be found, but they are remote; and though some of them have been brought to London, yet they are so dear, by reasons of the carriage, that few care to buy them.'*

Defoe was, of course, writing long before either the Leeds to Liverpool canal or the railways were built – both of which reduced transportation costs and made Wigan coal more widely available and affordable.

George Orwell, more than two centuries later, did not share Defoe's appreciation of the quality of cannel, describing it – indeed effectively dismissing it – in rather disparaging terms.

He had been watching local men, women and children 'scrabbling' for small pieces of coal from laden trucks on their way to the spoil heaps – a practice almost as old as industrialised mining itself. While some picked nuggets of coal from amongst the waste, others, he noted, found fuel in the shale trucks also on their way to the tip:

> *'If it is a shale truck there will be no coal in it, but there occurs among the shale another inflammable rock called cannel, which looks very like ordinary shale but is slightly darker and is known by splitting in parallel lines, like slate. It makes tolerable fuel, not good enough to be commercially valuable, but good enough to be eagerly sought after by the unemployed.'*

Many would disagree – the hydrogen-rich cannel coal was not only a sought-after, easy-burning domestic fuel but had also proved to be of great value, mixed with other coals, in the production of coke, a fuel which had become hugely important in the iron and steel industries. With increased mechanisation deep underground and improving

below: The railway yards at Blundell's Pemberton Collieries, showing some of the company's two thousand coal wagons. Photographed c.1931, this view was also sold as a postcard. The colliery's deepest shaft went 1,900 feet underground to the premium steam coal in the Orrell 4ft mine, and nearly 1,800 people were employed below and above ground. In the Wigan coalfield, the term 'mine' usually referred to the coal seam and not to the colliery. An explosion deep underground in the King Pit in 1877 had cost forty lives.

below: The last evidence of Wigan's deep mines were vast acreages of spoil heaps which dotted the landscape. These were removed in the 1970s and 1980s.

transport links on the surface, by the closing years of the 19th century the output of the collieries was so prodigious that Wigan itself was sometimes referred to as 'Coalopolis' – a nickname applied around the same time to mining centres in Australia, South Africa and America.

The quantity of coal brought up annually from Wigan mines grew throughout the period, peaking in the years just before the Great War. The figures were enormous – the Lancashire coalfields alone, of which Wigan's pits were a major component, yielded over 26,000,000 tons in 1907, about 10% of the total national production.

By the time the closure of the massive Bickershaw complex was announced, it was reportedly producing less than the commercially viable 1,000,000 tons a year. Bickershaw eventually closed in 1992, although most of the

others had gone decades before then. The last of the drift mines in the area – Quaker House Colliery – closed in the same year.

Open cast continued for a few more years but as the century drew to a close, applications to work open cast sites invariably ended in rejection on environmental and amenity grounds.

From the centuries during which the mining industry increasingly dominated the town and the surrounding areas, Wigan has been left with, amongst other things, some spectacular 'flashes' caused by subsidence and now landscaped into leisure areas, a network of pathways left by former mineral railways and a replica coal tippler on the towpath of the Leeds & Liverpool Canal – the 'physical' Wigan Pier. The mythical Wigan Pier, however, remains elusive and yet quite undiminished.

below: Even before the last of the deep collieries closed in 1992, some of Wigan's huge remaining stocks of coal were already being excavated at opencast sites throughout the Borough. These pictures show the scale of Raymin's Alexandra site in Whelley in the late 1980s. The size of the massive grab cranes in this photograph gives a sense of the depth of the workings.

WIGAN-
ON-SEA
"Rough Seas"

THAT ENDURING JOKE

'SOME PEOPLE SAY that there's a pier in Wigan town somewhere
George Formby said it led t'sands on stilts up in the air
Some folks'll say that it's a myth, but I don't think they're right
'Cos I once fell off yon Wigan Pier, staggerin' home one night.

I've taken part in catchin' tripe from waters deep and clean
You dangle mint balls on a string and hope that they are seen
By sticks of tripe that swim around, all shiny bright and new
And just to show where they come from, there's Wigan written all through

So if you're told that there's a pier in Wigan town somewhere
Don't laugh it off as others do – look round you'll see it there
It's spick and span and painted white and standin' out a mile
But if you're asked just where it is, don't say much, just smile.

chorus
It's long and it's strong and it leads nowhere
You can see it when the weather is clear
If you feel inclined and you've got the time
You can spend a lovely day on Wigan Pier.'

opposite page: Clevedon Pier in Somerset, photographed in the mist. It was seeing an elevated wagonway over Ince Moss in misty weather which, it is believed, led to the idea of the mythical Wigan Pier.

inset: One of several local photographers to capitalise on the fame of the mythical. Wigan Pier was James Blackburn in the 1920s and '30s. The 'seaside' views he offered were what every postcard buyer would expect from a seaside resort – a view looking towards Poolstock was captioned 'The Promenade'; the famous card of SS. *Thomas* was used to depict boat trips; an early electricity pylon near Pearson's Flash – erected when the National Grid was being established in the 1930s – became 'The Tower'; and other views of the flashes became 'Rough Seas', 'Moonlight' and 'Eventide'.

Wiganers are resilient people – and they were so long before their town became the butt of a joke. If the Wigan Pier joke did anything, it made the man in the Wigan street even more resilient, calling upon the deeply-ingrained local sense of humour to rise above the jibes, turn the joke on its

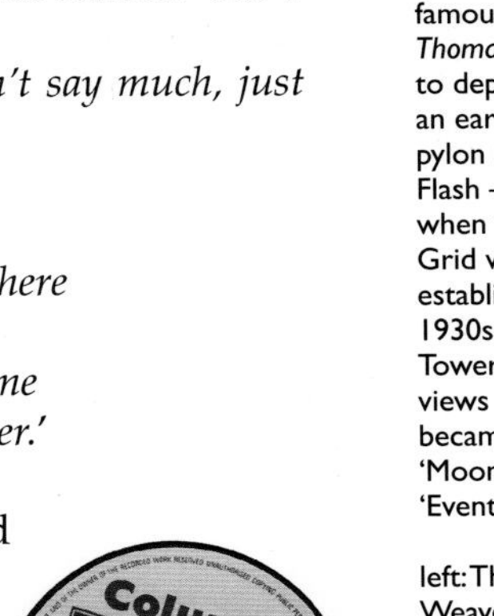

left: The Houghton Weavers recorded Jack Winstanley's song '*The Ballad of Wigan Pier*'.

right: Wigan-born George Formby is commemorated in the town by a statue in the Grand Arcade. For a time in 2014, the statue was removed as someone had deemed it a health and safety hazard but now it is back! The idea that Formby, even in statue form, presented a risk to public safety would have amused him, as he was more used to being considered – at least by some – an affront to public decency.

THE GEORGE FORMBY SOCIETY
GEORGE FORMBY OBE
1904-1961
ENTERTAINER AND FILM STAR
WAS BORN
NEAR THIS PLACE AT
3 WESTMINSTER STREET
26TH MAY 1904
WIGAN METROPOLITAN BOROUGH COUNCIL

above: A blue plaque marks the site of the Formbys' house at 3 Westminster Street – both the house and the street are long gone, the plaque now attached to a wall on Central Park Way. Music hall star George Formby Senior moved there when he bigamously married Eliza Ann Hoy in 1899 and his more famous son was born in the house on 26th May 1904.

head and feed it. The joke thus became Wiganers making fun of the seaside piers to which holidaymakers flocked in their summer thousands – but that take on the joke had much more to do with the three-foot long coal tippler than with George Formby's fanciful pier.

The delightful tongue-firmly-in-cheek lyrics which open this chapter are from Jack Winstanley's *'Ballad of Wigan Pier'* – recorded in 1980 by The Houghton Weavers – and are typical of that unique blend of irreverence and defiant ownership which the majority of Wiganers even today still feel towards the myth which has helped make their home town world famous. Jack's lyrics were just the latest in a number of songs, jokes and stories to draw on, popularise and even celebrate the idea of the pier.

The elder George Formby is generally credited with the initial popularisation of the seaside pier myth but his son, the banjolele-playing George Junior, also got in on the act, with references to it in at least a couple of his songs – *'On the Wigan Boat Express'* and *'Our Fanny's Gone All Yankee'*.

The former, one of his more risqué and innuendo-laden songs, was first recorded in 1940 and, perhaps surprisingly, was never actually officially banned by the BBC – although it probably did not get any radio plays either – while the less overtly suggestive *'With My Little Stick of Blackpool Rock'* was on the banned list.

In *'Our Fanny's Gone All Yankee'*, released in 1944, Formby told his audience that Fanny came from Wigan-by-the-Sea a name already featured in several spoof postcards.

The chorus for *'On the Wigan Boat Express'* imagined a pier so grand that it had its own railway terminus – and regular excursion trains bringing holidaymakers to enjoy the pleasures the pier promised:

'When we shunt, the back's in front
And the front part's in the rear.
If we survive, then we'll arrive
Alongside Wigan Pier.'

The idea that there might often have been a bit of 'hanky-panky' on the excursion trains which ran from the industrial towns to Blackpool, Southport and Morecambe is referred to in one of the verses

'Once a wedding pair didn't seem to care
They were full of love I guess
And the honeymoon started much too soon
On the Wigan Boat Express.'

H.V. Morton was wrong when he suggested that while Aberdonians knew how to capitalise on the worldwide fame their jokes gave them, Wiganers did not.

Wiganers, from the earliest days of the joke, poked fun at the idea, pandering to those who would wish to have a souvenir of their visit to the town – even if that was just a postcard of the tippler.

George Formby – An American 'cookie card' from 1937 *top*, a cigarette card from 1938 *middle* and a 1940s promotional photograph *bottom*.

above: An Edwardian publicity portrait of George Formby Snr.

right: The mythical Wigan Pier as imagined by seaside postcard publisher, Bamforth & Company.

below right: 'Wigan-by-the-Sea' another of the locally produced postcards – probably from the late 1920s – riding on the back of the joke and pandering to visitors who wanted to take home a memento of their visit. Although there is no name on the card, it is believed to have been produced by the prolific James Blackburn, a local professional photographer who had been in business in the town since 1903. He had a studio at 5 Birch Street, off Gidlow Lane, from 1903 until 1918, moving to 60 Scot Lane around 1919.

above: Two postcards of Southport, which had been visited by the group of miners on the train held up at Douglas Bank East signal box a mile from Wigan Wallgate station c.1891 (see page 90). George Formby Senior's music hall routine implied similar scenes could be enjoyed around Wigan's pier.

That wry sense of humour is still a deeply-rooted part of a Wiganer's character – as evidenced by the occasional white van seen parked in the town with a sticker on the back doors advising that '*No pies are kept in this van overnight*'.

Wigan, of course, had piers long before Formby's jokes, and while the actual piers were as far removed as they could be from the mythical structure celebrated in the music halls, the two remained quite distinct in local minds. Poking fun at, or pandering to, the idea of the mythical pier – and cashing in on it – became popular locally not long after the idea itself first became public.

The early years of the 20th century were the heyday of the picture postcard, so several enterprising local photographers produced souvenir cards of 'Wigan-by-the-Sea', offering typical 'seaside' views.

The origins of the idea of a seaside pier so far from the sea – a surreal, undoubtedly ridiculous and immediately

below left: Honiton Round Table in Devon organised an excursion train from Plymouth to Carlisle and back on 16th October 1982, and named it 'The Wigan Boat Express'. Seen here at Appleby station on its way north, the return journey followed the West Coast Main Line down through Wigan. That same year, a new marching tune, '*Wigan Pier*', was composed by A.R. Bennett at the Royal Military School of Music. Wigan Pier had certainly not been forgotten.

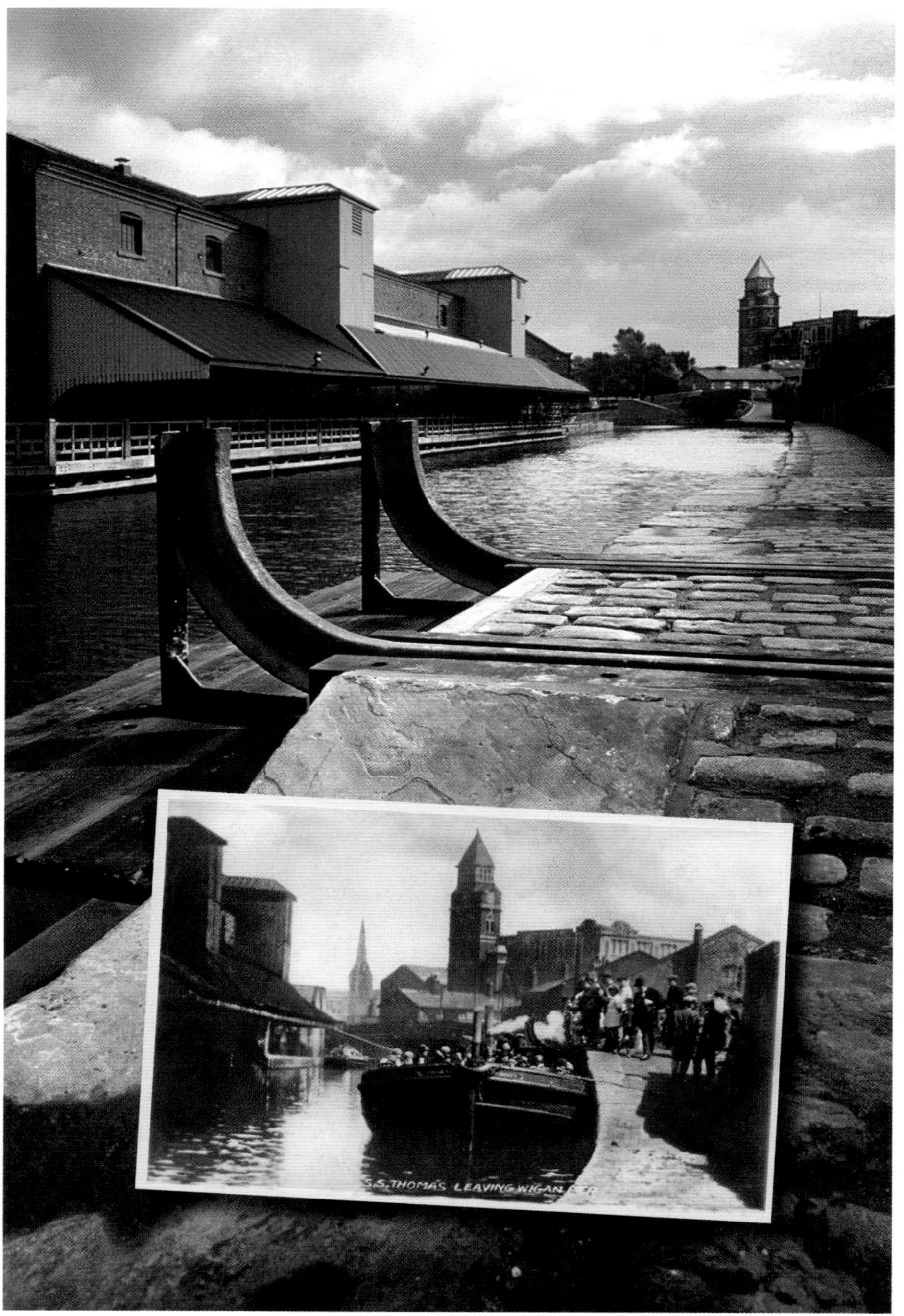
S.S. THOMAS LEAVING WIGAN PIER

opposite page: The replica tippler, photographed shortly after it was installed in the 1980s. Years of neglect since 2007, when the heritage centre closed, have left it to decay,

inset: James Blackburn's view of the steam barge SS *Thomas* loading passengers for a sail on the canal in the late 1920s – the curved rails were removed in 1929. For many Wiganers, a day's sail was the closest they got to a holiday. This card remained on sale well into the 1950s and it was re-published in the 1980s.

above: This card, published before 1920, may be the earliest to apply the 'Wigan Pier' name to the coal tippler known as Bankes's Pier. Clearly playing to the joke, the word 'Pier' is written within quotation marks suggesting that at this point it was still the 'so-called' Wigan Pier. An almost fully-laden steam-powered wide-boat is tied up just beyond the tipping mechanism.

funny idea – can be traced almost half a century before *'On The Wigan Boat Express'*.

It was certainly popularised by George Formby Senior, who developed stories about the mythical pier in his music hall act – but it is highly unlikely that he originated it. More likely is that he picked up on a comment he had overhead and realised its comic potential.

There are a number of versions of the story of the 'birth' of the idea. In the best known one, a group of colliers were returning from – or less probably, on their way to – the annual gathering of the Lancashire & Cheshire Miners' Federation on the beach at Southport, which attracted thousands of miners and their families from all over the region.

And the date that trip took place? Well, that has been suggested as anytime between 1891 and 1897, when huge

left: The electric waterbus *Emma* on the canal in spring 2003 – the 21st century equivalent of SS *Thomas*.

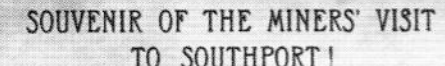

Lightbown, Southport

" Toilers too 'gainst Nature's forces great,
" We Welcome You! With trawls and baited lines
" We drag from mighty treacherous deep her wealth,
" Whilst you, coney-like, beneath the verdant earth
" Burrow for dusky diamonds—England's strength.

" Sunny Southport began its mild career
" With such as we! Now, Garden City famèd!
" Viewing with pride our beauteous healthy town,
" We reckon nothing lost, but trebly gained
" That to friends our offspring we can lend. E.D.D.

miners' gatherings took place on Southport sands – local tradition has the summer of 1891 as being the most likely.

James Booth Lawler would have been just 16 years old in 1891 and he would not adopt the name George Formby until 1897. It seems probable, therefore, that the idea of Wigan Pier was already current long before he popularised it in his illustrious music hall career.

Most versions of the story agree that it was a misty day and all agree the train was held up at the Douglas Bank East signal box less than a mile outside Wigan Wallgate station on the Southport to Manchester line.

The more credible version – if indeed any of them is actually credible – has one of the

above: This late 19th century souvenir of the Southport miners' gala included verses to both fishermen and colliers, who were all '*toilers too 'gainst Nature's forces great.*'

right: While pleasure cruises from seaside piers were taken aboard well-appointed paddle steamers, cruises from 'Wigan Pier' were on open barges.

travellers being awakened as the train jolted into motion after being held up at signals and asking *'Where the b----y h--l are we?'* and getting the response from one his companions *'Just by Wigan Pier'*. If he was jolted awake, then the more likely time of day would be the return trip from Southport in the evening as dusk and mist started to obscure the view from the railway carriage.

opposite page top: Passengers leaving the Excursion Platforms – only used in the summer months – at Blackpool's Talbot Road station c.1904 (*left*), and on the excursion platform at Morecambe station (*right*).

So what prompted the suggestion that Wigan had a pier? The colliers, returning from Southport, which very definitely *did* have a pier, would doubtless also be familiar with the piers at Blackpool and Morecambe – regular destinations for Wiganers going on holiday during Wakes Week. Many excursion trains left Wallgate station for Southport and North Western station for Blackpool and Morecambe, as thousands made their annual pilgrimage to those three resorts.

But a pier in Wigan? That really was a piece of original thinking but what might have evoked those associations with Southport?

Not far from where the train had come to a halt at the Douglas Bank signals, there was a long wooden gantry stretching into the distance which carried a waggonway across the Leeds & Liverpool Canal, the River Douglas and the surrounding low-lying flood plains.

It was used for moving trucks laden with coal from Lamb & Moore's Newtown Pit to their Meadow Pit. In total, it ran for about two thirds of a mile and enabled those loaded coal trucks to be rope or chain-hauled to the rail heads near Frog Lane.

The waggonway had only recently been erected – having been brought into service in 1889 or 1890 – and so it would still have been a new and visually interesting addition to the Wigan landscape when that 1891 trainload of miners saw it looming out of the misty dusk.

Given the lasting impact which that gantry had, and still has, on the image of the town, it is remarkable that, apparently, not a single photograph of it seems to have survived.

Was photographing it – and exploiting its fame or infamy commercially – perhaps

SOUTHPORT?
NOT B••••• LIKELY!
THIS 'ERE IS
WIGAN PIER!

below: A cartoon recreation of the train stopping at the signals in 1891 adorned the side of the actual signal box, part of *The Way We Were* exhibition.

In the years before the Great War, George Formby Senior was at the height of his popularity and Wigan Pier was already well known to just about anyone who went to the music halls – but as far as Wigan's postcard publishers were concerned, neither the canal nor the 'pier' were considered to be amongst the town's major attractions.

already considered a civic *faux pas* within just a few years of the birth of the joke? Wigan photographers had already established commercial markets for photographs of all aspects of the town and its collieries, mills and other industrial areas before the end of the 19th century and would continue to do so throughout the Edwardian era, so this is a significant gap in their surviving record.

Whether or not any photographs of it were ever taken is another question to which we may never know the answer and so, by the same token, is any sense of exactly what it might have looked like – although the use of cable-driven or rope-driven waggonways was widespread and their construction probably followed a fairly similar pattern.

On that basis it is possible to make plausible suggestions as to what sort of appearance the structure might have had. Given that it was, in part at least, a rope or chain-hauled system in the 1890s, there would almost certainly have been engine houses at strategic points along the way – a single engine-and-rope combination could not have operated over a length of around 1,200 yards. For significant lengths of the route, the system used a gentle slope and gravity to move the full coal trucks along – but on those slopes the stationary engines provided essential braking as well as a haulage system to pull the empty wagons back up the inclines.

An engine house or winding house positioned alongside or even on top of the gantry might very well have looked

After the tippler was demolished in 1929, most postcard companies – perhaps not aware of its removal – simply continued to use their earlier views of the canal with 'Wigan Pier' in place. Indeed, some cards showing the original tippler were still being issued into the late 1960s. One exception was the Scarborough publisher E.T.W. Dennis, who either sent a photographer to capture the changed view, or carefully retouched the tipping mechanism out of their view. The top postcard was published around 1936 and showed the scene on the towpath which George Orwell would have encountered on his quest for the pier. To add to his confusion about whether or not the pier actually existed, numerous postcards of it were still on sale in the town. The lower view had first been published in the 1920s, and was simply tinted for the later market. It remained on sale well after the Second World War.

like the pavilions found on seaside piers further adding to the visual similarity with a pleasure pier rather than a working railway.

The location of the gantry – a long way from the Wigan Basin – poses several interesting questions, not least of them being when did the name 'Wigan Pier' move from Formby's fanciful idea to become associated with the little tippler on the canal? On the basis of surviving evidence, a date somewhere around 1920 seems to be likely.

The Lamb & Moore gantry had no connection with the canal at all, delivering coal to a rail head. It was a 'pier'

purely in the realms of fantasy but what an engaging and enduring fantasy it has proved to be.

The gantry was demolished c.1910, to be replaced by conventional rail links, so it had a life of little more than twenty years – the mythical Wigan Pier has already outlasted it by more than a century.

But when did the tipplers – perhaps ten or more – which delivered wagons of coal from around the Wigan coalfield into waiting barges at the canalside become known as piers and when did Bankes's Pier – the derelict replica of which stands on the canalside today – become known as Wigan Pier?

above: Blackpool Tower and beach. This late 1890s *Photochrom* print was part of a series sold as summer holiday souvenirs. To get his audience to link the shape of Lamb & Moore's gantry with the familiar profile of a structure like Blackpool's North Pier was all part of Formby's routine. North Pier, the resort's oldest, had opened in 1863, and the tower in 1894.

By the 1930s and '40s, little more than a quarter of a century after it had been dismantled, there appears to already have been some considerable confusion as to where the structure which inspired the music hall Wigan Pier had actually stood. Even George Orwell had the wrong story, confusing Bankes's Pier with the mythical Wigan Pier. It was certainly Bankes's Pier he went in search of in 1936 but then he would hardly have gone looking for the mythical pier about which he clearly knew absolutely nothing.

On the BBC Overseas Service just before Christmas 1943, a question which had been posed by two soldiers – Sergeant

right: Trestle piers – like Great Yarmouth's Britannia Pier seen here c.1897 – could be found all around the coastline of Victorian England.

Salt and Signalman McGrath – was read out by the BBC's Australian-born presenter Colin Wills, who had sought the answer from no lesser an oracle than Orwell himself.

As part of the show, in which people sought to pose unanswerable questions, the two soldiers had asked *'How long is the Wigan Pier?'* and *'What is the Wigan Pier?'*

Might their question have been asked somewhat tongue-in-cheek? Were they asking about the mythical pier rather than the physical one? If that was the plan, it went over the heads of both Wills and Orwell.

Wills responded *'Well, if anyone ought to know, it should be George Orwell who wrote a book called* The Road to Wigan Pier. *And here's what he's got to say about it.'*

Sadly, Orwell's response was typically uncharitable as far as Wigan was concerned – painting a picture of the town which even those who knew how depressed the area was would not have immediately recognised – but by 1943 Orwell's name in the town was already even muddier than his description of the canal. His answer to the question which had been asked by the two soldiers – and which was probably asked as a joke in itself – was also completely inaccurate:

top: Seen at a Wigan fairground.

above: Seaside postcards like these would have been familiar to Edwardian Wiganers from their annual holidays in Blackpool. George Formby Snr's stories were designed to endow his mythical Wigan Pier with the same trappings of summer holiday fun.

> *'Well, I am afraid I must tell you that Wigan Pier doesn't exist. I made a journey specially to see it in 1936, and I couldn't find it. It did exist once, however, and to judge from the photographs it must have been about twenty feet long.*
>
> *Wigan is in the middle of the mining areas, and though its a pleasant place in some ways its scenery is not its strong point. The landscape is mostly slag-heaps, looking like the mountains of the moon, and mud and soot and so forth. For some reason, though it is no worse than fifty other places, Wigan has always been picked on as a symbol*

Both George Formbys – father and son – are buried in Warrington's Manchester Road cemetery, their final resting place marked by a magnificent marble tombstone. The curtains and columns which frame George Snr's bust were modelled on the proscenium arch of one of the Manchester music halls in which he regularly performed. Eliza, wife of George Snr and mother of George Jnr, was buried there in 1981

of the ugliness of the industrial areas. At one time on one of the muddy little canals that run round the town, there used to be a tumble-down wooden jetty; and by way of a joke, someone nicknamed this Wigan Pier. The joke caught on locally, and then the Music Hall comedians got hold of it, and they are the ones who have succeeded in keeping Wigan Pier alive as a by-word, long after the place itself has been demolished.'

Of course one of those who had *'picked on'* Wigan as a *'symbol of the ugliness of the industrial areas'* was Orwell himself – which is dealt with in the next chapter of this book – but what of those music hall comedians *'who have succeeded in keeping Wigan Pier alive'*?

While he didn't invent the idea, George Formby Senior is the man usually credited with introducing stories of a seaside pier in Wigan to music hall audiences.

He first appeared on the music hall stage as George Formby in the closing years of the 19th century – although he had been performing since he was a boy – and, like every other touring comedian, needed a gimmick or two to make his act distinctive.

He quickly learned that just a mention of Wigan Pier was sufficient to get audiences rolling in the aisles – and that fact alone should dispel any suggestion that Wiganers, initially at least, had failed to see the humour of it all. They had no problem whatsoever with laughing at the contradiction between the fact and the fantasy such a story evoked.

It is worth mentioning at this stage that Formby did not tell jokes about Wigan Pier, he concocted humorous monologues about it. He was a master at conjuring up the impossible. A popular line from his shows suggested:

'It's very nice is Wigan Pier. Ah've been there many times in my bathing costume and dived off th' high board in

t'water. Next time you go on holiday to Wigan, make sure you visit t'pier.'

below: John Willie's Ragtime Band's audience at Wigan Pier – had either actually existed – would have been the mill girls who would 'give a cheer', and the colliers whose real intention was, according to the song, to find the nearest bar.

Just when the idea came about that the pier was on the canal is unclear but anyone who knew the typical depth of a canal would certainly also have found the idea of a *'high board'* anywhere near the towpath hilarious in itself.

Not that seaside piers usually had high boards either but why let a little inaccuracy spoil the bizarre image such a remark must have conjured up.

Formby is said to have introduced the idea of the pier initially to audiences in and around Wigan – where he lived at the time – so the humour and incongruity of the town having a seaside pier, not to mention being a holiday resort, would not have been lost on anyone who lived and worked in the area.

At this point, we have to recognise the genius of the man – he seems to have told one group of 'Wigan Pier' stories when performing for local audiences and another quite different set when talking to audiences further afield. That would suggest that the essential idea of the pier evolved quite quickly into a sophisticated and multi-dimensional creation.

Wigan audiences got one-liners which played on their knowledge of where the mythical Wigan Pier was supposed to be, making them party to the joke and thus adding an additional level to the humour which grew out of that shared complicity.

London audiences, on the other hand, simply needed an idea of where Wigan was – 'up north' and far from the sea – in order to be amused by the very idea of it having a pier.

right: The Grand Hippodrome Theatre in King Street as it looked when George Formby Senior first appeared on its stage. This postcard dates from c.1905. The theatre was built in 1904 as the New Theatre & Hippodrome and could seat more than 1,250 people. As well as both George Formbys, others who performed there over the years included Charlie Chaplin and Gracie Fields.

To achieve that, he had to change his stage persona a little for the two different audiences.

In Wigan his stage character seems to have been something akin to the typically ill-informed, tap-room philosopher, while for the more sophisticated London audiences, he presented himself as the simple, gullible northerner in ill-fitting clothes, apparently well out of his comfort zone – which, of course, was about as far from the truth as it could be.

Singing songs such as *'I'm not quite so daft as I look'* – which he also recorded on both wax cylinders and 78rpm records – enhanced and perpetuated that idea.

The area around Lamb & Moore's gantry was prone to flooding so, after a bout of wet weather, he was guaranteed a laugh if he introduced his act by telling his audience that on his way to theatre that night he had *'passed Wigan Pier and the tide was in'*. Only locals 'in the know' would have seen the humour in that observation.

Formby's stage act reputedly included both stories and songs about the pier, all intended to draw on memories of a typical seaside holiday with bathing costumes, bands playing, funfairs and

below: A tinted postcard c.1904, of the Tivoli Music Hall in London's Strand, where George Formby Senior opened his act as one of his many alter egos, 'The Wigan Sprinter'.

perhaps even candy floss, so to non-Wigan audiences, the idea of the tide coming in around a seaside pier would not, on its own, be funny. Only if you knew the geography of the area in which the mythical pier was said to have stood, would you chuckle.

There had been a pier at Southport since 1860, Blackpool since 1863 – like many others, originally serving as a landing stage for coastal paddle steamers. There were more than a hundred other similar piers around the coast, so a pier with its pavilion at the end had been part of the seaside holiday experience for the entire lifetime of most of his audience.

Once the idea of Formby's Wigan Pier had been embedded in the minds of his music hall audiences, Lamb & Moore's elevated tramway which had inspired it was no longer

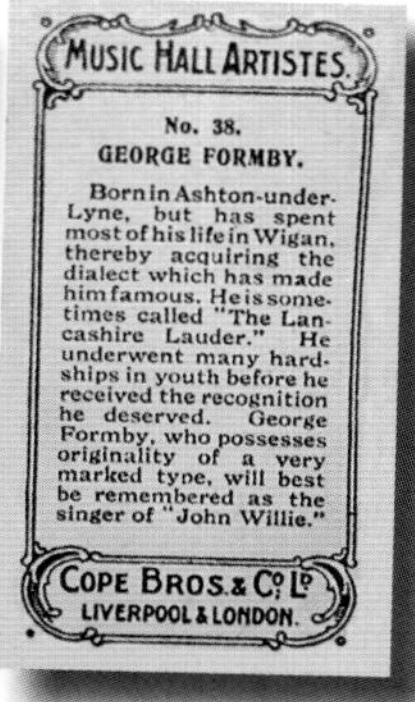
MUSIC HALL ARTISTES.

No. 38.
GEORGE FORMBY.

Born in Ashton-under-Lyne, but has spent most of his life in Wigan, thereby acquiring the dialect which has made him famous. He is sometimes called "The Lancashire Lauder." He underwent many hardships in youth before he received the recognition he deserved. George Formby, who possesses originality of a very marked type, will best be remembered as the singer of "John Willie."

COPE BROS. & Co. Ld.
LIVERPOOL & LONDON.

above: From a cigarette card series celebrating stars of the music hall, c.1905, Gorge Formby Snr is seen here much more smartly dressed than any of his stage characters.

Marie Lloyd *(left)*, Little Tich *(below left)* and George Robey (*below right*), were just three of George Formby Snr's contemporaries on the music hall circuit. Marie Lloyd and Little Tich both appeared on the same bill as Formby on several occasions, including a period at London's Tivoli Music Hall. These portraits of Tich – real name Harry Relph – appeared in the magazine *Black and White Budget* in 1902. The photographers of both performers, Foulsham & Banfield, operated their studio in London's Wigmore Street.

LITTLE TICH : THE WONDER OF THE WORLD

above: An advert for a late-model Edison phonograph. The wax cylinder was already in decline when Formby made his first recordings.

central, or even integral, to the story. Indeed, as it had been demolished long before the fame of Formby's pier even reached its peak, its actual existence would have been quite unknown to most.

Formby's pier was a place where the locals supposedly flocked in search of fun and relaxation. To underline its claimed local popularity, in *'John Willie's Ragtime Band'*, recorded in 1917, the chorus ran:

'Hear us when we play on Wigan Pier
The mill girls flock around and give a cheer
And the colliers all shout 'by gum, 'ear, 'ear,'
'Mine's a beer, mine's a beer, mine's a beer'.'

'John Willie' was one of his most popular stage characters, a name apparently not chosen at random. The character is said to have been named after Formby's friend, the Wigan-born song-and-dance man John William Jackson, one of the members of 'The Eight Lancashire Lads', a popular music hall act formed in the mid 1880s, amongst whose members at different times were both Charlie Chaplin and, much later, Nat Jackley. History does not record if John Willie Jackson was as gormless as Formby's John Willie. Chaplin is said to have first performed with the group in 1900 at the age of just ten.

With many membership changes, they continued to work the halls well into the 1920s, long after George Formby Senior had died.

The character of John Willie re-appeared several times in Formby's recordings – *'John Willie come on'*, *'Send for John Willie'* and several others – a number of which were also later re-recorded by his son.

His 'John Willie' stage persona and appearance were designed to make him appear simple and gormless – which he clearly was not – wearing trousers which were baggy and too big, and a jacket which was several sizes too small. To cap it off, he wore a

below: The character of John Willie achieved worldwide fame as Charlie Chaplin's baggy-trousered little man, and is kept in the public eye today by street artists and 'living statues'. Here, the familiar figure of 'Chaplin' – albeit wearing John Willie's trilby – adjusts his make-up in a small square near the Grand Canal in Venice.

trilby hat and had his boots on the wrong feet. Replace the trilby with a bowler and what do you get? Charlie Chaplin – while working for Fred Karno – modelled his little man on 'John Willie', initially wearing clothes which he had borrowed from Formby.

above: Charlie Chaplin in a publicity shot from *City Lights*, made in 1931.

John Willie was, however, just one of the characters he introduced to his audiences. Sometimes he was billed as'The Lancashire Lauder' or 'The Wigan Sparrow' and sometimes as his most unlikely character – given his life-long ill-health – 'The Wigan Sprinter'.

The carefully choreographed character of the 'Wigan Sprinter' seems, like so many of his creations, to have been a rather simple and gullible one – someone who saw the trivial achievements of his life as significant milestones. It was a persona he used regularly and he even had photographs taken of himself in character, and publicity cards produced. Anything less like a sprinter would be hard to imagine.

On many London billings he was simply 'The Man fra' Wigan', the name given both to one of his songs and a monologue.

Once he had made the big time, Formby would open his act to London audiences with the line '*Good evening, I'm George Formby fra' Wigan, I've not been in England long*', playing on the commonly-held belief that Londoners knew little, if anything, about 'up north' or about the rigours and hardships of life in the industrial centres of Lancashire and Yorkshire – it might as well have been a different country.

He certainly was poking gentle fun at Wigan and his northern roots, while also pandering to southern prejudices – and laughing all the way to the bank in the process – but he was doing so in an affectionate manner, and one which his audiences, both north and south, clearly enjoyed.

below: A publicity card for Formby's 'Wigan Sprinter' character probably produced around 1912.

GEORGE FORMBY,
The Wigan Sprinter.
SHOWING PRIZES HE HAS WON

above: George Formby Snr's '*John Willie's Ragtime Band*' was issued on Zonophone's 'The Twin' label – denoting that it was a double-sided disk. Their earliest recordings were single sided, and ran at 85rpm. On the other side was '*Bits Fra' Wigan*'.

above right and right: Wigan Infirmary around the time the Formbys moved to Malvern House – given George's persistently poor health, living next to the hospital was perhaps not such a bad idea.

below: Malvern House, the Formby's home on Wigan Lane as it looks today, now occupied by Wigan Royal Infirmary's post-graduate library.

After George Senior's death, George Junior took over the John Willie character and costume – eventually abandoning the costume but developing the character as his own. He even starred as 'John Willie' in two films – *Boots, Boots* and *Off the Dole* in 1934 and 1935.

Contemporary accounts tell us that George Formby Snr stood apart from most music hall comedians – whose acts could, perhaps, best be described as 'bawdy' – in that he always presented what audiences of the day considered to be a 'family show'.

When he died in 1921, his obituary in *The Times* alluded to that fact by noting that *'his humour was often crude, and always simple, but it was always true humour, and, what is more, it was invariably clean.'* In music halls those were rare qualities.

John Willie might have been the mouthpiece George Senior used to launch his surreal idea of a Wigan Pier but not even he could have imagined its enduring fame – or indeed that the idea of such a structure would play such a significant role in the history of the town itself.

There appears to have been no malice inherent in his stories about the town and its fictional pier, and his Edwardian audiences would never have assumed that there was any. It would never have been his intention to brand the town with a label which, by association, would later be used to epitomise the very depths of urban squallor.

The bitterness about the very idea of the pier, which engulfed both town and townsfolk, would not take hold until after Orwell's book.

No, George Formby's Wigan Pier was conceived as an affectionate flight of fancy. It was an idea so ridiculous that even Wiganers could laugh at it – and along with it – without in any way feeling demeaned or ridiculed by it. After all, he lived in the town, and was dependent on music hall audiences both locally and nationally for his celebrity.

Alienating his local Wigan audience would not have been a sensible thing to do and doing so would certainly have provoked a local backlash.

As his fame increased, the family moved progressively up the housing ladder but still based in Wigan or its immediate surroundings.

From their humble beginnings in Marsh Lane and later Westminster Street, they had moved up-market, first to a fine terraced house on Dicconson Street and, by the outbreak

above: More sophisticated than the card illustrated on page 82, these James Blackburn postcards date from 1937, just after Orwell's visit. In the upper card, five views are of Pearson's Flash – one captioned '*Not Orme's Head*' lest anyone mistake the spoil heap for the North Wales landmark. The sixth view shows the Duke of Gloucester at Wigan Pier in 1937. The second card featured more views of Pearson's Flash, Top Place, and the pier. These cards remained on sale well into the 1950s, helping to keep the jokes alive.

right: Formby's northern audiences would have been regular visitors to local resorts such as New Brighton, Blackpool, Morecambe and Southport, so his stories about Wigan's brightly-lit seaside pier would have painted a familiar picture.

below: Harry Lauder was the highest paid performer on the music hall stage by some margin before George Formby Snr hit the big time. Early on in his career, Formby was often billed as the 'Lancashire Lauder'. Lauder's crooked cane was a familiar part of his act, and an idea which Formby borrowed – later loaning his cane to Charlie Chaplin.

of the Great War, they were living in a large detached villa, Malvern House, adjacent to Wigan Infirmary – perhaps not a bad place to be living, given George's persistent and worsening ill-health.

An elegant property on Wigan Lane was a public show of George Formby's growing affluence and a far cry from the humble house in Marsh Lane, off Water Street in the town centre – the home of Eliza's parents – into which the newly and bigamously married Formby, using the name James Booth, had moved in August 1899.

This affluent address, and the string of racehorses which George owned by that time, were both clear evidence that Wigan Pier – along with his many other music hall routines – and his songs and gramophone records, had been very good to the family.

George was quick to realise the potential of the phonograph and had cut his first wax cylinder in 1906 – for Louis Sterling – when he recorded *'The Man from Lancashire No. 2'*, the first of a total output of approaching 200 recordings on both wax cylinders and 78rpm records. This was the second of his *'Man from Lancashire'* songs, the earlier version only being recorded three years later in 1909.

Louis Sterling had moved to Britain from America in 1903 as the manager of the British Zonophone recording company but

had left in the following year to establish his own short-lived recording company.

That later recording of *'The Man from Lancashire'* was issued on a 78rpm record for the Zonophone company, with whom Formby had signed a contract two years earlier and on whose label most of his subsequent recordings were issued. Sterling was by then working with the Gramophone Company which would, in 1911 take over Zonophone, – the group later becoming HMV and eventually EMI. Indeed, the label on Formby's last Zonophone recording – *'Don't fall out with your husband'* coupled with *'I'm not so daft as I look'*, issued in 1921 – includes 'Nipper' the HMV dog looking into the horn of the gramophone.

So, by the time the family moved to Wigan Lane, he was already a well-established recording artist.

Although the songs were at the heart of his recordings, they were often only part of the performance, with Formby ad-libbing as he went along – much like he did in his stage act – with comments to the recording engineer filling the same role as his familiar banter with the orchestra conductor during his live theatre performances. Surprisingly, none of his recordings, as far as records show, were of songs specifically about Wigan Pier.

top: Like Lamb & Moore's gantry at Wigan, Dunston Staithe on the Tyne – the biggest wooden structure in Britain – carried a colliery railway, in this case to deliver coal to waiting ships. It ran out across coal-blackened sands just as in Weston and Lee's song.

above: A postcard, c.1920, of the coal staithes at Dunston-on-Tyne.

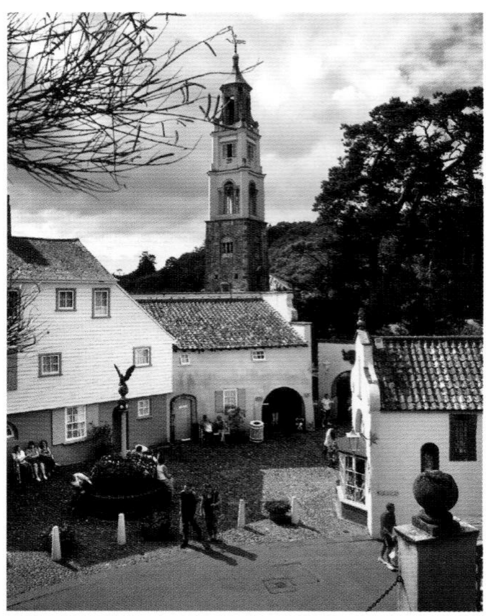

The Italianate village of Portmerion, which Clough WIlliams-Ellis started to design and construct in 1926, was every bit as much a flight of fancy as the Wigan Pier he referred to in his essay in *The Spectator* in 1930.

By 1917, the family's eighteen years of calling Wigan 'home' came to an end when they moved to Warrington.

George Jnr was already away in Ireland – he had been shipped off to the Curragh, two years earlier at the age of eleven, to become an apprentice jockey.

His father, whose cough had been a part of his act for years and was already in rapidly declining health, would die four years later at the age of just 45.

Throughout the first half of the 20th century, and long after George Senior's death, the idea of Wigan Pier remained – in the minds of many both locally and nationally – up there with the most memorable of associations, its existence or non-existence unquestioned.

Stories and songs about it by Formby and others were still sufficiently well known – and obviously still widely performed – for them to be referred to in newspapers almost a decade later. For example, the pier was clearly familiar enough to the readership of *The Spectator* magazine in 1930 for it to need no explanation. The celebrated architect Bernard Clough Williams-Ellis – creator of the Italianate village of Portmerion in North Wales – writing in the magazine on 1st February that year, acknowledged the pier's legendary status in a piece entitled 'Plumbers or Poets?', when he wrote:

> *'Berlin sings about its avenue of linden trees; Aberdovey about its bells (which are mythical), and Wigan about its pier, which it valiantly invented, as it would have had to invent anything else that it could sing about with any pride or affection. Save, of course, its own indomitable citizens. For its pathos and wry humour,* 'Wigan Pier' *can only be matched by a few of the War-time marching songs compounded of cynicism and heartache. Only intolerable conditions can produce such songs. English industrial towns produce them.'*

THE CALEDONIAN RAILWAY
BLACKPOOL
EXCELLENT TRAIN SERVICE FROM CALEDONIAN STATIONS. CHEAP TOURIST TICKETS.
For Holiday Literature and all Information apply at the Booking Office.

So Ellis attributed the invention of Wigan Pier not to Formby but to the Wiganers themselves – adding that it was something they could sing about 'with pride and affection'. He referred to *'Wigan Pier'* within quotation marks, clearly implying that it was a song title – but to which song was he referring? Certainly not to George Formby Junior's celebrated innuendo-laden ditties, which did not appear until more than a decade later.

References to Wigan Pier in any of Formby Senior's songs are difficult to find – there's *'John Willie's Ragtime Band'*, of course, but little else. Music hall historians have searched long and hard for transcripts of any songs about the pier which he might have sung but have come up with nothing.

It would seem, therefore that while the town and its mythical pier featured in many of his monologues, like most of his contemporaries his act was never scripted in the formal sense of being written down and delivered word-for-word at each performance. That means that there exist only scant records of just what his Wigan Pier stories might have contained. Most of it was kept in his head and thus the detail of the individual stories has largely faded from memory.

above: Typical railway posters advertising the delights of Blackpool and Skegness, published pre-1922.

Songs about the pier were indeed written – one notable example was by Robert Patrick Weston, best known for such standards as *'I'm 'enery the Eighth I am'*, *'When Father Papered the Parlour'*, *'Paddy McGinty's Goat'*, *'The Lion and Albert'* and *'With Her Head Tucked Underneath Her Arm'*.

Weston's *'Wigan Pier'*, co-written in collaboration with Robert 'Bert' Lee, was published in April 1922.

However, rather than coming from Wigan itself – and thus with first-hand experience of the *'intolerable conditions'* in northern industrial towns of which Clough Williams-Ellis would write – Weston, real name Robert Patrick Harris, came from Islington in London and Lee was a Yorkshireman.

George Formby's fanciful creation of Wigan as a holiday resort, complete with bathing machines and donkeys, was celebrated in *The Way We Were*, the heritage centre at Wigan Pier. This photograph was taken in 1987.

This must surely have been the song to which Ellis was referring – with its irreverent and tongue-in-cheek lyrics it seems to chime perfectly with his remarks. Despite their lack of a local pedigree, Weston and Lee managed to encapsulate the fundamental characteristics of Wigan humour in a song which, while still portraying Wigan as a 'must visit' holiday destination, tells of a pier far as far removed from Formby's stories as it could possibly be.

Formby's Wigan Pier – and Jack Winstanley's which was its direct descendant – stretched out across golden sands and was located somewhere along the sunny coastline of pure fantasy. The tippler long celebrated as Wigan Pier on the other hand, is rooted in the world of utilitarian necessity.

Weston and Lee's mythical pier stood somewhere quite different, neither entirely real, nor entirely fiction. While still clearly set in the realm of the improbable, it is slightly less fanciful than Formby's pier – several obvious references to the 'real' Wigan making it just that little bit more imaginable.

It was still recognisable as a seaside pier – and the lyrics draw on the improbability of Formby's flight of fancy – but the choruses place it in the blighted and relentlessly bleak industrial landscape of 1920s north-west England.

While the verses are in the spirit of Formby and offer the same unlikely advice – that Wigan Pier is better than Blackpool, better than Southport and better than Morecambe – the choruses are about the real Wigan and not always very flattering about it at all.

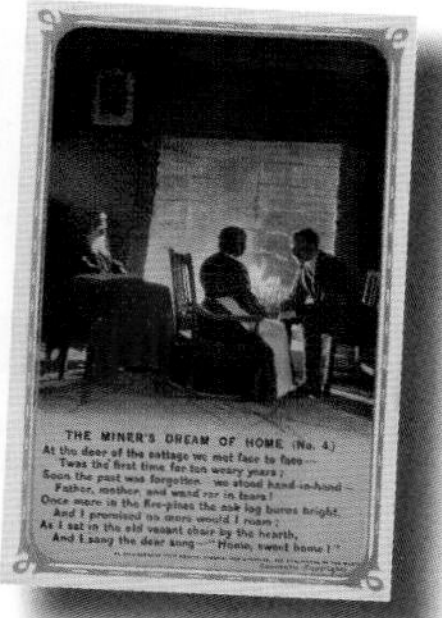

The Miner's Dream of Home, by Will Godwin and Leo Dryden – mentioned in Weston & Lee's song – told of a miner, returning home after a decade working abroad, to an England which only ever existed in such songs. It appeared on numerous Edwardian postcards.

The original inspiration for Weston and Lee's pier may have come, not from Wigan, but from the giant wooden coal staithes stretching out into the sea on the north-east coast of England. Indeed, some survive to this day and their visual similarity to seaside piers – from a distance at least – is unmistakable.

There, the beaches were blackened with a mixture of coal spilled from the wagons travelling overhead and dust settling on the sands as the coal was discharged into the holds of waiting ships.

Such a description could also have been applied to the area beneath Lamb & Moore's gantry in Wigan and also to the landscape around the town's many canal-side coal tipplers. Staithes may have looked like piers but they were strictly utilitarian. As one of choruses suggested:

'All the shingle there is black,
Worth half-a-crown a sack
So coom, coom, coom to Wigan Pier.'

Wigan is still presented as a popular holiday resort, with the opening verse, firmly tongue-in-cheek, setting the tone.

'On ev'ry hoarding nowadays each railway company
Will tell you where to spend your annual holiday by the sea
For 'Skegness is so bracing' so the adverts all declare,
And Blackpool's beautiful, if you can afford the fare.
But where's the earthly paradise, with blue Italian skies,
The Naples of the North, the place they never advertise?'

The *'place they never advertise'* was,

above: Workmen in the process of demolishing the original Bankes's Pier – later known as Wigan Pier – in 1929. The announcement that the demolition was to take place prompted the *Manchester Guardian* to publish its lament *'A Wigan Fairy Tale'*.

according to the song, *'the favourite beauty spot in Lancashire'*:

'They've no donkeys by the brine,
But the whippet-racing's fine
So coom, coom, coom to Wigan Pier.

Why walk a mile at Southport just to paddle your poor feet?
In Wigan when it rains you'll find a puddle in ev'ry street.
Why go to Douglas fishing? it's a swindle and a sell
On Wigan Promenade there's fish and there's chips as well.
Why listen to them singing 'Coal Black Mammy' by the foam?
Go where the coal-black daddies sing 'The Miner's Dream of Home'.'

A beach, a promenade and coal mines – a fanciful Wigan of extreme contradictions. Formby would have approved of that as well.

Just seven years after Weston and Lee's song was published, the decision was made in 1929 to demolish the now redundant Bankes's tippler – by which time so famous was 'Wigan Pier' that it generated national coverage.

The *Manchester Guardian*'s *'Wigan Fairy Tale'* has already been recounted earlier in this book but the newspaper was by no means alone in its interest in the passing of the, by then redundant, little cast-iron tippler which had – in the absence of the 'real thing' – become an iconic and internationally renowned landmark.

This was the heyday of the cinema newsreel and the demolition of Wigan Pier aroused interest from British Pathé, one of the country's leading newsreel companies.

Their short silent film of the demolition – at just one minute and eleven seconds in length – showed the dismantling of the tippler being undertaken on a cold morning in December 1929, just a few months before Ellis would write about its fame.

In the film, clouds of steam are seen rising from the warm waters of the canal, while a Sentinel steam lorry from Calderbanks scrap merchants stands ready to cart away the ironwork, the event watched by a small crowd of local men and boys. The film was shown in newsreels nationally – so presumably also in Wigan cinemas – in early 1930, with the title '*The end of Music Hall's oldest joke*' and sub-headed '*Wigan Pier – there really was a pier! and it's 50 years old!!! – demolished*'. So they dated the origin of the original pier jokes and of the tippler itself, to the late 1870s.

Neither date was correct – Meyrick Bankes's tippler was much older, the three and a half mile 4 foot gauge railway from his Winstanley collieries to the Pier Head at Wigan having been laid in 1845, while the first references to Wigan Pier certainly did not appear before 1891.

And was it, in fact, an end to music hall's oldest joke? Manifestly not as, in 1929, George Formby Junior and his banjolele hadn't even really got started with the idea. As *The Manchester Guardian* had written just before the event, '*What do they know of Wigan Pier who say it can be dismantled?*' History would prove Pathé wrong and *The Guardian* right.

Trying to rid the town of the legacy of Wigan Pier jokes is no recent thing; as early as 1927 – just a year after H.V. Morton had written about the value of capitalising on the idea – articles were being written on how to kill the joke off once and for all.

None of them managed to either dent the pier's enduring fame, or assuage the civic fear that Wigan was being laughed at rather than laughed with.

Reported in a newspaper article – published in Singapore and headed '*Killing the Wigan Pier Joke*' – the President of the Lancashire and Cheshire branch of the British Medical Association Dr E. Hodkinson Monks, himself a Wiganer, offered its annual meeting in the town some sound historical reasons why the mere mention of Wigan should not provoke a chuckle –

below: Scholes Bridge, once the site of Wigan's 18th century spa.

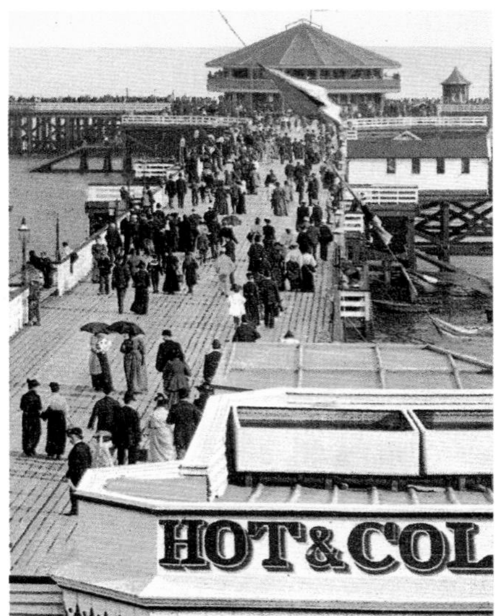

Clacton Pier in Essex, seen here over the Hot & Cold Sea-Water Baths in 1897 – as familiar to George Formby Senior's London audiences as Southport and Blackpool piers were to his northern fans. 'Hot & Cold' perfectly describes the attitude of successive Wigan Councils towards the mythical pier over the past 125 years.

while conceding that the town's name *'has been a Music Hall gag throughout the country and even in the Dominions for many years'*.

Describing it as *'this much-maligned town'* – a decade before George Orwell ever came on the scene – he echoed John Hilton's accounts of Wigan's 18th century spa waters which had been published three years earlier.

In the course of his speech, he surprised his audience by presenting a fascinating reversal of the story they might have been expecting. The newspaper reported that:

> *'It seems almost like a Music Hall joke to-day to talk about Blackpool sending visitors to Wigan, but a century and more ago it was customary for coaching parties to be organised at Blackpool in order to drink the waters at Wigan Spa, it being the fashion at one time to favour inland watering-places rather than seaside resorts. Dr. Monks quoted the following reference to the Wigan Spa from a directory for the year 1797, preserved in the Wigan Public Library:– 'The Wigan Spa or the New Harrogate', as it is called, is described as a strong sulphurous water, recently discovered in boring for coal in a field near Scholes Bridge.*
>
> *There has been erected a very elegant building for the use of those who resort to the spring with conveniences for drinking the water, or for using it either as a hot or cold bath.'*

Interesting but Dr Monks' attempt to kill the pier joke was clearly unsuccessful. In fact he actually did his own little bit to perpetuate it, by giving every member of his audience there a postcard of Wigan Pier – Bankes's coal tippler – to take home with them, just two years before it was dismantled. Trying to kill off Wigan Pier is a futile exercise. Far from being forgotten, the pier continues to be celebrated to this day.

left: Graham Farish's 'N' gauge model of No. 31421, the Class '31' diesel locomotive 'Wigan Pier'.

When the heritage centre was at the height of its popularity in the 1980s and '90s, limited edition model cars and buses adorned with the Wigan Pier logo were available and, in 1993, Regional Railways named one of their 1959-built Class '31 locomotives' *Wigan Pier*. Two model railway companies – Lima and Graham Farish – produced 'O' and 'N' gauge models of it respectively. The locomotive itself, sadly, was scrapped in 2007.

above: A scale model of a Model T Ford, van complete with 'Wigan Pier' signage.

below: The cover of the 2004 Hodder Paperback edition of Jasper Fforde's 2003 fantasy novel *The Well of Lost Plots*.

New jokes about the pier still surface occasionally – a popular one during a spell when the local rugby league club was, untypically, performing well below par being:

'Police have found the body of a man near Wigan Pier wearing a Wigan rugby shirt, women's underwear, fishnet stockings, suspenders and lipstick. They have removed the rugby shirt to save the family from any embarrassment.'

The pier also crops up more recently in Jasper Fforde's 2003 '*Thursday Next*' series fantasy novel *The Well of Lost Plots* – for which Fforde created, and then quoted from, a wonderfully humorous fictitious biography of George Formby Junior's life – the biography said to have been written by an equally fictitious biographer, '*John Williams*' – the name perhaps coming from Formby's John Willie?

According to 'Williams', when many of the rich and famous were alleged to be fleeing wartime Britain in 1942 for safe havens overseas, George and his wife Beryl told the press that they would remain steadfast and fight the Nazi invaders until '*the last bullet on the end of Wigan Pier*'. At the end of

above and right: The Wigan Pier Fish n' Chips restaurant in Squamish, a suburb of Vancouver in British Columbia, Canada, has been welcoming customers – amongst them visitors from Britain and ex-pats – since 1994. It is run by a Wiganer.

right: One of the Wigan Pier bars in Tenerife even copied the 1980s logo from the Wigan Pier heritage site.

the war and in recognition of his wartime heroism, George was allegedly made lifetime non-executive President of a Republican England.

The comic appeal of Wigan Pier has now endured for 125 years and remains, it seems, quite indestructible – which is more than can be said for the replica of Bankes's tippler.

Hearing what both George Formbys, father and son, would have had to say of the joke's longevity would be well worth a listen.

It may never have had George Senior's high diving board, nor have been '*the favourite beauty spot in Lancashire*' of Weston and Lee's song and it certainly did not stretch out a mile across golden sands as Jack Winstanley's affectionate song suggested but its fame still stretches out much further than any of the 'real' piers which inspired it.

The Pavilion Picturedrome in Library Street first opened its doors as a roller rink before being converted into a cinema in 1910. It regularly showed newsreels before the main feature, so would almost certainly have shown the Pathé film of the demolition of the tippler in 1929.

At one point years ago, there reportedly was a white-painted jetty in Hawaii with 'Wigan Pier' painted along its side. Until recently there were two competing Wigan Pier bars in Tenerife – now there is one – and there is a Wigan Pier fish and chip shop, sweet shop and pie shop in Squamish in British Columbia, run by an ex-pat Wiganer who even supplies his celebrated pies to local supermarkets.

As recently as 2003 in Henderson, Nevada – a town more than 250 miles from the sea – Wigan Pier Drive was chosen as the name for a street in a new residential development.

In Turkey and in Spain there are British-themed Wigan Bars – no mention of the pier but the Wigan name in itself is a tourist magnet.

Wigan Council have realised – for a second time in the last thirty-five years – that the mythical Wigan Pier is not going to go away and accepted that its name is undoubtedly the town's most instantly recognisable asset.

But just how the history and legacy of both the real and the mythical Wigan Piers are going to dovetail into the future of the canalside 'Wigan Pier Quarter' remains unclear. At the time of writing, little seems to have been decided.

Had H.V. Morton's advice been heeded ninety years earlier – that the burghers of Wigan should follow the example of their Aberdonian counterparts, embrace the jokes about the pier and exploit them, advice given a decade before George Orwell's jaded view of the town was published – who knows how differently Wigan might be spoken of today.

Had the legacy of the mythical pier been celebrated for the past 125 years we would certainly have a much more complete picture of the stories and jokes with which George Formby Senior regaled his audiences and that really would have been wonderful.

THE ROAD TO WIGAN PIER

GEORGE ORWELL'S BOOK *The Road To Wigan Pier* is not a book about Wigan Pier. Indeed, it is only partly a book about Wigan. Rather, it was intended as an indictment of a succession of British governments which had done little to reduce unemployment, ameliorate the effect of low wages on the working classes, or alleviate poverty.

In Orwell's mind, it was a clarion call for social justice made at a time when Fascism was gaining sway across much of Europe.

Wigan, and Wigan Pier, barely got a mention – apart from in the book's title, of course – and the mention it did get was little more than a rebuttle of a claim made by the *Manchester Guardian* that:

> *'Set down in Wigan or Whitechapel, Mr Orwell would still exercise an unerring power of closing his vision to all that is good in order to proceed with his wholehearted vilification of humanity.'*

opposite: A collier making his way up Standishgate in 1932. Miners in flat caps with their snap tins and billy-cans, and mill girls in clogs making their way to and from work were a common sight on Wigan's streets.

above: On a low stone plinth opposite a Lidl car park, this plaque commemorates Orwell's brief stay in Wigan. Most of the buildings and streets with which he would have been familiar were cleared away in the 1970s and 1980s.

left: Orwell lamented that Wigan's environs were dominated by slag heaps, coal mines and grime. By the late 1980s, almost every trace of the coal industry had been landscaped out of sight, save for a few open cast sites around the perimeter of the town and small working drift mines.

top: Orwell's research involved reading back issues of the town's newspapers in the reference library – as depicted in a postcard c.1925, *top*. The interior of the building, designed by Alfred Waterhouse, remained little changed until the 1970s and the upper floor now houses the local history library, *above*.

He responded to what he considered to be a slight with a measure of what he believed to be legitimate indignation:

'Wrong. Mr. Orwell was 'set down' in Wigan for quite a while and it did not inspire him with any wish to vilify humanity. He liked Wigan very much – the people, not the scenery. Indeed, he has only one fault to find with it, and that is in respect of the celebrated Wigan Pier, which he has set his heart on seeing. Alas! Wigan Pier had been demolished, and even the spot where it used to stand is no longer certain.'

Bearing in mind that he had earlier insisted that he *'liked Wigan very much – the people, not the scenery'*, his account of his quest for the pier on a cold March day, makes grim reading, with very little to suggest that he found anything about the town which he liked at all:

'I remember a winter afternoon in the dreadful environs of Wigan. All round was the lunar landscape of slag-heaps, and to the north, through the passes, as it were, between the mountains of slag, you could see the factory chimneys sending out their plumes of smoke. The canal path was a mixture of cinders and frozen mud, criss-crossed by the imprints of innumerable clogs, and all round, as far as the slag-heaps in the distance, stretched the 'flashes' – pools of stagnant water that had seeped into the hollows caused by the subsidence of ancient pits. It was horribly cold. The 'flashes' were covered with ice the colour of raw umber, the bargemen were muffled to the eyes in sacks, the lock gates wore beards of ice. It seemed a world from which vegetation had been banished; nothing existed except smoke, shale, ice, mud, ashes, and foul water.'

The ground floor of Waterhouse's Victorian Gothic building now houses the Museum of Wigan Life. It had opened in 1878 as the Library & Reading Room. Across Rodney Street to the left was Wigan's rather unassuming Town Hall – not for Wigan the flamboyance of the town halls in Bolton, and elsewhere – while up Library Street to the right, was the 1903-built Wigan & District Mining & Technical College, now the Town Hall.

However accurate that description might have then been, there were many other places in industrial Britain at least as grim. The flashes were rarely still, seldom stagnant – the winds which often swept across them made sure of that – and Wigan could hardly be blamed for the weather in what was, in 1936, a bitterly cold winter.

Several areas of industrial London could have then been described in a remarkably similar vein but that would not have supported his pre-determined thesis that it was 'up north' where the real poverty and hardship existed.

It is easy to understand the resentment Wigan folks felt towards how their town was painted in the book – a resentment which still persists. Wiganers have long memories!

So how did Wigan finish up as the archetype for everything that was bad about Northern industrial towns? Why not *The Road to Bradford, The Road to Barnsley* or *The Road to Rotherham*?

There was, however unfair, an obvious logic to Orwell's choice of title for the book – the fame of Wigan Pier was already national, even international, and the incongruous juxtaposition of a mythical seaside pier in a northern right: Just a few survivals of the once typical Wigan terraced street – with a mill at the end – can still be found in the town today.

above: A recreation of the kitchen hearth in a worker's house of the 1920s and '30s. For most, living conditions had not improved for decades and for many they had deteriorated as wages failed to keep pace with rising prices – a timeless story.

industrial town miles from the sea was, in the minds of many, an idea almost beyond surreal. At the time, he even admitted that his decision to spend time in the town, and use the pier in the book's title, was largely because of Wigan Pier's enduring fame. Everyone already knew of the pier and the book's title was thus endowed with immediate recognition.

If he could build upon that incongruity – even exaggerate it a bit

The Orwell floodlit and reflected in the mirror-still waters of the canal on a summer's evening in 1985 – before the clock tower was added.

left: A machinist in one of the workshops at Park Forge, early 1930s. The town's many engineering and mining companies required and maintained a large skilled workforce, even in times of economic depression.

left: A group of blacksmiths pose for the camera around their anvil at Park Forge in the early 1930s.

by painting as bleak a picture of Wigan as possible – his journalistic intuition would have led him to see the potential for emphasising just how bad things 'up north' really were.

It must be remembered that he was not writing for the people of the north, let alone the people of Wigan. He was writing for a largely south-eastern readership made up of armchair-socialist intellectuals whose righteous indignation, if fanned sufficiently might, he believed, be awakened to the need to do something about the widening gulf of inequality in 1930s Britain.

Wigan Pier was no more central to his thesis than the frozen flashes, or the tripe and pigs' feet to which he sometimes referred. It was simply a label, a hook, a pointer, an already familiar lure which he hoped would encourage people to read what he had to say. So, perhaps George Formby Senior bears more responsibility for Wigan's unfortunate reputation than George Orwell.

The impact which his depiction of the living conditions beneath the chimneys of the '*dark satanic mills*' of industrial towns might have on the people of the north-west in general,

above: One of James Blackburn's 1930s postcards of Wigan's spoil heaps and flashes.

right: Was arriving in Wigan in winter, when living and working conditions were at their most harsh, part of Orwell's original plan? Despite exploring the town during his March visit, he ignored any of its positive aspects. This view of the Victorian pavilion in Mesnes Park, with clean white snow, paints a very different picture to his impression fifty years earlier that '*everywhere there were mounds of blackened snow*'.

opposite page top: Pemberton Colliery's 1932 carnival float.

middle: A tug of war at a miners' gala, mid 1930s.

bottom: Girls at May Mills, Pemberton, c.1935, with their patent knot-tying machines.

and Wigan in particular, probably never crossed his mind.

Orwell was primarily a journalist – and a very successful one although he is probably better known today for novels such as *1984* and *Animal Farm* – and like all journalists, he was not averse to embellishing his essays to increase their impact. It follows, therefore, that only the worst of Wigan would completely serve his purpose.

He certainly seems to have sought out the worst – it has been alleged that he first lodged with John and Lily Anderton at 72 Warrington Road but moved because their house was insufficiently squalid.

His quest for squalor was at odds with his stated aims that he:

> '*... wanted to see what mass-unemployment is like at its worst, partly in order to see the most typical section of the English working class at close quarters.*'

Instead of finding '*typical*' board and lodging, he sought out disgusting digs – conditions which would yield a narrative likely to revolt most of his readers and perhaps even make them grateful for the fact that their own life experiences were so very different.

He could, perhaps, have stayed with a typical working class family and get a first hand honest account of how they lived, the standards they endeavoured to maintain, and the hardships and shortages with which they had to juggle. He did

above: The men's swimming pool was covered over each winter and used as a dance, concert and boxing venue.

above right: The Empress Ballroom in Station Road, with its celebrated sprung dance floor, was built by the Atherton brothers in 1916. It was still used as a ballroom into the 1970s, although by then it was known as The Casino. The building achieved its greatest fame in the late 1970s as the venue for Wigan's famous – to some locals, notorious – Northern Soul 'All-nighters'. This postcard dates from around 1920. The building was demolished in 1983.

not. Instead he chose an extreme example with which to repel his readership, presenting it as typical.

He certainly did find somewhere which met his purposes, although the living conditions he described – in what must have been one of the town's worst boarding houses – were far removed from the typical conditions under which even the poorest of Wiganers lived. The setting was the Brookers' tripe shop and lodging house in nearby Sovereign Road where the lodgers slept four in a room, surrounded by filth.

Orwell presented it as typical, citing as evidence the fact that the other lodgers didn't seem to complain – save for a commercial traveller for a tobacco company who stayed one night and, after remonstrating with the Brookers that this was not the sort of accommodation he was used to, packed his bag and moved elsewhere.

Orwell did not enlighten his readers as to how long he put up with it himself but eventually even he had had enough – and having described himself as coming from a '*lower-upper-class*' background, he probably stayed there only long enough to experience just how bad things could be. That happened one morning after breakfast when he too packed his bags, presumably having filled his notebook with sufficient anecdotes to meet his journalistic requirements:

> *'On the day when there was a full chamber-pot under the breakfast table, I decided to leave. The place was beginning to depress me. It was not only the dirt, the smells, and the*

above left: Wigan was by no means unique in having slum dwellings in the 1930s. Indeed, living conditions similar to those which Orwell described were still to be found in towns and cities right across Britain – and the Empire – decades after *The Road to Wigan Pier* was published. This small terraced house living-room/kitchen in Susannah Place in Sydney, Australia was occupied until the early 1970s but had hardly changed since the 1920s. The entire row of houses is now preserved – unrestored – as a museum.

above: Harry Williams' garage in the early to mid 1930s. The vehicles on the forecourt are marked as 1928, 1928 and 1930 models. He also ran the Wigan Pier Service Station on Pottery Road near Wigan Pier.

vile food, but the feeling of stagnant meaningless decay, of having got down into some subterranean place where people go creeping round and round, just like blackbeetles, in an endless muddle of slovened jobs and mean grievances.'

That he had volunteered to experience such squalor is quietly overlooked. And again, Wigan was not unique. Such horrors could just as easily have been found less than a mile from his '*lower-upper-class*' home, or from the fictitious pub, *The Moon Under Water*, in the lounge bar of which he would later claim to drink, to write and to read his newspaper.

Orwell's upbringing certainly did not chime with his socialist views. His dislike of the class system was driven in part by guilt that he had enjoyed a privileged childhood which others could never experience but simply spending a few days in a disgusting boarding-house in Wigan – or anywhere else for that matter – could never expiate that guilt.

Just how he actually felt about working class life in general, and subjecting himself to the horrors of the Brookers' lodging house in particular, has to be considered against the experiences of his own life.

His inability to relate to the people whose lives he set out to understand must have made his time in Wigan challenging – not helped by the crisp upper-class accent with which he spoke.

The sense that '*Tha's not fra' around here?*' would have been only too obvious to anyone with whom he tried to engage. Not that he arrived in Wigan totally inexperienced in mingling with what he had been brought up to believe were the underclasses. He had spent time, dressed in rags,

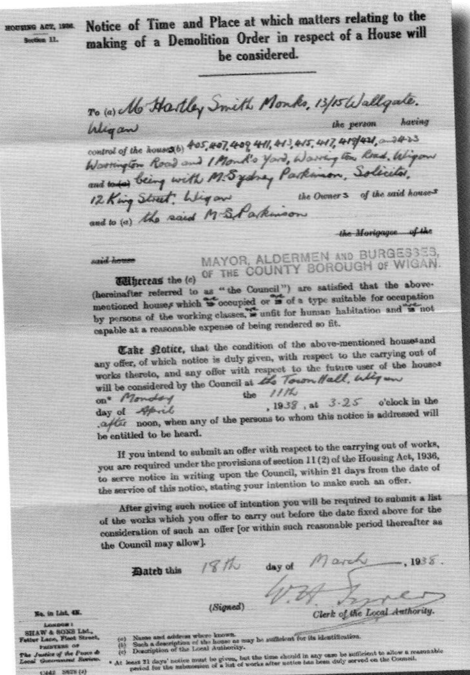

HOUSING ACT, 1936. Section 11.

Notice of Time and Place at which matters relating to the making of a Demolition Order in respect of a House will be considered.

To (a) Mr Hartley Smith Monks, 13/15 Wallgate, Wigan the person having control of the houses (b) 405, 407, 409, 411, 413, 415, 417, 419/421, and 423 Warrington Road and 1 Monk's Yard, Warrington Road, Wigan and ~~to (a)~~ being with Mr Sydney Parkinson, Solicitor, 12 King Street, Wigan the Owners of the said houses and to (a) the said Mr S. Parkinson ~~the Mortgagee of the said house~~

Whereas the (c) MAYOR, ALDERMEN AND BURGESSES, OF THE COUNTY BOROUGH OF WIGAN (hereinafter referred to as "the Council") are satisfied that the above-mentioned houses which are occupied or are of a type suitable for occupation by persons of the working classes, are unfit for human habitation and are not capable at a reasonable expense of being rendered so fit.

Take Notice, that the condition of the above-mentioned houses and any offer, of which notice is duly given, with respect to the carrying out of works thereto, and any offer with respect to the future user of the houses will be considered by the Council at the Town Hall, Wigan on* Monday the 11th day of April, 1938, at 3.25 o'clock in the after noon, when any of the persons to whom this notice is addressed will be entitled to be heard.

If you intend to submit an offer with respect to the carrying out of works, you are required under the provisions of section 11 (2) of the Housing Act, 1936, to serve notice in writing upon the Council, within 21 days from the date of the service of this notice, stating your intention to make such an offer.

After giving such notice of intention you will be required to submit a list of the works which you offer to carry out before the date fixed above for the consideration of such an offer [or within such reasonable period thereafter as the Council may allow].

Dated this 18th day of March, 1938.

(Signed)

Clerk of the Local Authority.

No. in List, 4K.

LONDON: SHAW & SONS Ltd., Fetter Lane, Fleet Street, PRINTERS OF *The Justice of the Peace & Local Government Review.*

(a) Name and address where known.
(b) Such a description of the house as may be sufficient for its identification.
(c) Description of the Local Authority.
* At least 21 days' notice must be given, but the time should in any case be sufficient to allow a reasonable period for the submission of a list of works after notice has been duly served on the Council.

Notification of a hearing to consider the imposition of a Demolition Order for eleven houses, considered to be '*unfit for human habitation*', issued in March 1938. The issue of such an order was the first stage in the legal process, under Section 11 of the Housing Act 1936, to empower the council to clear away the town's worst slums.

living rough in the East End of London and in the less salubrious areas of Paris.

His London lodgings would not have been all that different to the worst he found in Wigan, and he had tramped the roads of England with beggars, all to try and immerse himself in what he saw as the 'real' culture of the under-privileged.

Despite his best efforts, he was totally out of his comfort zone in the impoverished towns and inner cities of Lancashire and Yorkshire.

Educated at Eton – Aldous Huxley was one of his tutors – he came from a background where the level of hardship endured by the people he met in London's East End, in the Paris slums, and in Wigan, Barnsley and Bradford was completely beyond his imaginings. Even as he experienced those hardships, he could always remind himself that, unlike those he wrote about, he could just walk away at any time of his choosing.

Writing about such conditions was something with which he was already familiar by the time he arrived in Wigan to start work on *The Road to Wigan Pier*. His earlier attempts at exorcising his upper class upbringing – by 'roughing it' in London and Paris – had been described in his 1933 book *Down and Out in Paris and London.*

Although the town gets mentioned here and there throughout the book – but mainly at the beginning – by the end of the first chapter, Mr Orwell was already on a train from Wallgate station heading east, making notes in which he attempted to place his recent experiences within an historical context.

His picture of Wigan was one-sided, narrowly focused and included only those aspects of the town which supported his central thesis.

He never visited a working men's club, never attended a rugby league match, never visited working-class houses with their clean white front steps – a clear sign that there was a clean house within – and in fact never did any of the things which essentially defined the lives of honest hard-working Wiganers.

Rather than being an impoverished backwater where everyone suffered, Wigan was, like any town, a mixed bag. Yes, there were intolerable hardships and poverty but there were also rich opportunities. The town offered many skilled jobs and excellent opportunities, both through apprenticeships and the training courses available at the Mining & Technical College.

Creativity was not being ignored either – Wigan had established one of the first art schools in the country as early as the late 1850s.

The new college buildings in Library Street, opened thirty years before Orwell's visit, were equipped to the highest standard, and were already nationally famous as a centre of excellence for their training courses in mining, engineering and building. The top floor, with its large north-facing roof lights, had been specially designed as art studios.

Orwell left the town without mentioning any of that:

'The train bore me away, through the monstrous scenery of slag-heaps, chimneys, piled scrap-iron, foul canals, paths of cindery mud criss-crossed with the prints of clogs. This was March, but the weather had been horribly cold and everywhere there were mounds of blackened snow. As we

above: Despite the hatchet job he did on Wigan, Orwell is remembered in two pubs – *The Orwell* at Wigan Pier, now closed, and *The Moon Under Water* in the Market Place, named after the fictitious London pub in which he claimed to read his newspaper and write his essays.

below left: Ice on a frozen puddle on the canal tow-path.

below right: Piles of scrap-iron are still a feature of the view from trains leaving Wigan – and indeed from most other industrial towns.

Orwell ignored anything of beauty or value in Wigan which might undermine his thesis. Standing next to the parish church, the town's war memorial, erected in 1925, was designed by the eminent architect Sir Giles Gilbert Scott, whose other works included the design of Liverpool's Anglican Cathedral, Battersea Power Station and the iconic red telephone box.

moved slowly through the outskirts of the town we passed row after row of little grey slum houses running at right angles to the embankment. At the back of one of the houses a young woman was kneeling on the stones, poling a stick up the leaden waste-pipe which ran from the sink inside and which I suppose was blocked. I had time to see everything about her – her sacking apron, her clumsy clogs, her arms reddened by the cold. She looked up as the train passed, and I was almost near enough to catch her eye. She had a round pale face, the usual exhausted face of the slum girl who is twenty-five and looks forty, thanks to miscarriages and drudgery; and it wore, for the second in which I saw it, the most desolate, hopeless expression I have ever seen.'

Even for an experienced journalist, that is rather a lot to deduce from just the briefest of glances from a passing train, and contains a number of conclusions which were not drawn from his experience of Wigan but were based on assumptions informed by his existing beliefs about the lives of the working classes.

Generations of Wiganers might refute his claim that clogs were clumsy – they were, after all, the everyday footwear of tens of thousands of people – and in a town of red-brick terraces, most if not all of them blackened by the soot of thousands of chimneys, both domestic and industrial, the homes he saw would certainly have been anything but grey.

Despite his publicised rejection of his own background, and all his prior experiences living with the under-privileged, his understanding of the everyday existence of others fell well short of being fully formed.

In Chapter 9 of *The Road to Wigan Pier,* he as much as admitted the impossibility of his ambition to become truly

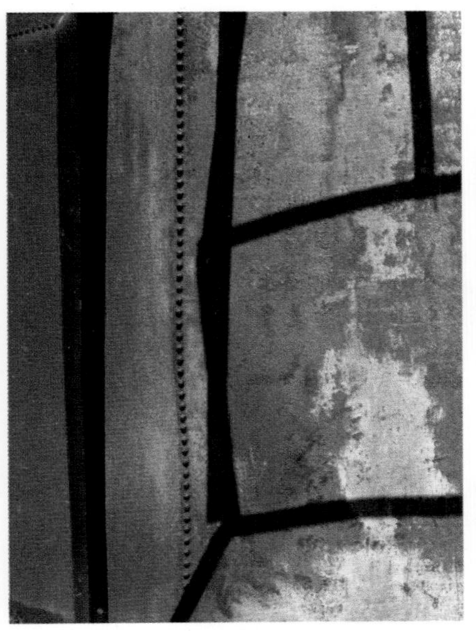

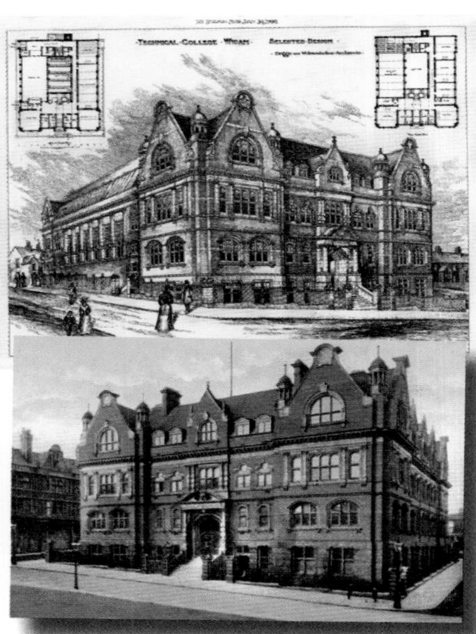

Socialist and empathise with the working classes, when he weighed his current leftish leanings against the baggage he admitted that he would always carry:

> *'When I was fourteen or fifteen I was an odious little snob, but no worse than other boys of my own age and class. I suppose there is no place in the world where snobbery is quite so ever-present or where it is cultivated in such refined and subtle forms as an English public school. Here, at least one cannot say that an 'English' education fails to do its job. You forget your Latin and Greek within a few months of leaving school – I studied Greek for eight or ten years, and now, at thirty-three, I cannot even repeat the Greek alphabet – but your snobbishness, unless you persistently root it out like the bind-weed it is, sticks by you till your grave.'*

From the comfort of his railway carriage, as the train set off from Wallgate station on its way towards Manchester and at a safe distance from the lives of the people with whom he had singularly failed to engage, he sought to explain the genesis of what he had just experienced, blaming:

above: Briggs & Wolstenholme's winning design for Wigan Technical College in Library Street was featured in *The Building News* in July 1900 and celebrated in Edwardian postcards. As Wigan & District Mining & Technical College, it reflected the town's prowess in mining education, and by the time of Orwell's visits, its courses and students were very highly rated. The elegant building is now the Town Hall.

above left: Rusting water tanks at Gidlow Washeries. Investment in the Wigan and Standish coalfields continued into the 1960s.

right: H.R.H. The Duke of Gloucester's barge, named *Duke of Gloucester* in his honour, having passed the site of the demolished coal tippler, makes its way towards Wigan Basin during the Royal Visit to the town's Boys' Club in 1937. The barge had been specially commissioned and fitted out in readiness for taking members of the Boys' Club on canal sailing holidays.

below right: Members and staff of Wigan Boys Club on board the *Duke of Gloucester* returning back down the canal after the Duke himself had disembarked.

'... the one-eyed scoundrels of the nineteenth century [who] *praised God and filled their pockets; and this is where it all led – to labyrinthine slums and dark back kitchens with sickly, ageing people creeping round and round them like blackbeetles. It is a kind of duty to see and smell such places now and again, especially smell them, lest you should forget that they exist; though perhaps it is better not to stay there too long.'*

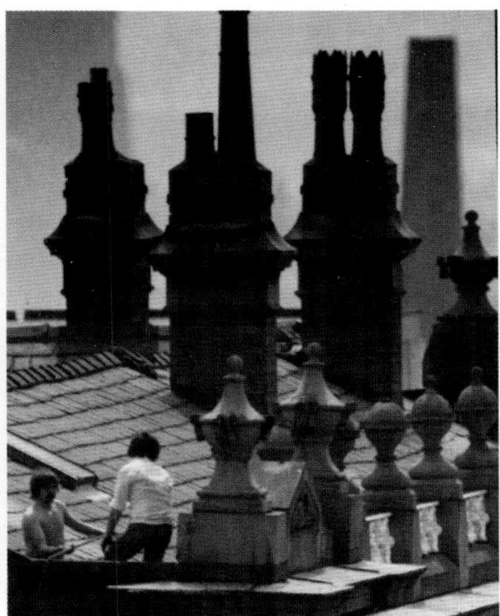

above: Wigan rooftops, with one of the chimneys of the now-demolished Westwood Power Station in the distance.

above left: Little London, a narrow close off Standishgate seen here c.1910, was typical of the high density housing still to be found in and around the town centre at the time of Orwell's visit to Wigan.

Comments like that added strength to the accusation in *The Manchester Guardian* that he had *'an unerring power of closing his vision to all that is good in order to proceed with his wholehearted vilification of humanity'*.

Only a few pages into the book there was already little if any evidence to support his published assertion that *'He liked Wigan very much – the people, not the scenery'*. Those were the same people who were roundly accused by him of lacking even the most basic hygiene, of smelling awful and, by implication, of all living in slums.

He had focused on the worst of Wigan – which was certainly no more typical of the town as a whole than was the best of Wigan – but the latter would have certainly been equally worth looking at if his intention had ever been to present an honest and objective impression of the town.

John T. Hilton's 1934 *Wigan Town and Country Rambles* – published less than two years before Orwell's visit – paints a very different picture of the town. Neither account is impartial of course but the contrast between the two is both fascinating and vivid.

While Orwell focused his attention on the worst slums, poor health, and what he saw as a down-trodden and utterly dejected population living in conditions which were

'The Wilds of Wigan. Ha! Where is it?' – a locally produced postcard from the early 1930s, showing the blighted landscape of Wigan's coal industry of which Orwell would later write *'A slag-heap is at best a hideous thing, because it is so planless and functionless. It is something just dumped on the earth, like the emptying of a giant's dust-bin. On the outskirts of the mining towns there are frightful landscapes where your horizon is ringed completely round by jagged grey mountains.'*

the antithesis of civilised human existence, Hilton saw much in the town to be worthy of comment and praise, devoting much of his book to describing and promoting it.

Hilton's Wigan must have seemed a much more attractive place in which to live and work than Orwell's – but by then he had moved to Wigan to live and would have become more familiar with the town's qualities:

> *'The town possesses an excellent water supply; a modern installation for electric current, an up-to-date and regular Motor-bus service and control, linked with all the*

below right: In sharp contrast, other postcard publishers sought to present an altogether different view of the town. This postcard of Mesnes Park was probably published the year before Orwell's visit – its scene a far cry from the *'monstrous scenery of slag-heaps, chimneys, piled scrap-iron, foul canals, paths of cindery mud criss-crossed with the prints of clogs'* of which he wrote – presented a face of the town which Orwell ignored. Any truly objective account of Wigan should have included both.

principal routes of the country, Gasworks, Parks, Markets, Baths, Libraries, Infirmary, Sanatoria, Tuberculosis Dispensary, Technical College, Grammar School, Girls' High School, and a growing number of elementary schools, with a department for School Clinics, but it has not, as yet, we regret to say, a Museum and Art Gallery, which would lend a mighty inspiration to the town, as the Mining and Technical College has done, and is still doing, through the outstanding generosity, and the voluntary activities of our public-spirited townsmen, for the technical and artistic training of the community far and wide.'

To read *The Road to Wigan Pier*, however, is to read an account of a town where there was little education, no culture and few, if any, saving graces. To admit to any such institution as a popular museum would have seriously undermined his thesis, preferring instead to simply ignore anything which might suggest that the town had any merits, or the people any redeeming qualities.

John Hilton also drew attention to the borough's on-going building projects aimed at replacing sub-standard housing, clearing vast acres of semi-derelict slums and improving the living conditions of the growing workforce,

above and below left: Just a decade before Orwell's visit, the town's museum – already a treasure-house of objects from the Stone Age to the present time – had been bequeathed a stunning collection of Egyptology from the estate of Sir John Scott, a Wiganer born in Standishgate, who had pursued an eminent career in the law and who is credited with reforming the legal system of Egypt. The collection of ancient grave goods was given to him by the Egyptian Government, in thanks for all his services. In 2015, Scott's collection was the subject of an exhibition in The Museum of Wigan Life. He had been knighted in 1894 and died in 1924.

above: Not long after the publication of *The Road to Wigan Pier*, enterprising local postcard publishers were already seeking to dispel the image Orwell had presented of the town – although the '*What you expect*' image was absolutely typical of what anyone arriving in the town by train would first encounter. Orwell's agenda, of course, meant he had no interest in the '*What you see*' views of Mesnes Park and The Plantations.

by building some of the largest council housing estates in the country.

> *'Whole colonies of dwellings have been erected at Beech Hill, Bottling Wood and Spring Bank; also at Orrell, on an area of land off Orrell Road close by the Pemberton boundary line.'*

Another feature of Hilton's account was that he also listed many of the clubs and societies – membership of which, he noted, was open to *'all classes'* – including football, rambling, bowling, cricket, and running.

Indeed, Wigan's Boys' Club was sufficiently well known to be included in a tour of boys' clubs undertaken by Prince Henry, Duke of Gloucester, in 1937, the same year that Orwell's bleak indictment of the town was published.

Amidst considerable civic flag-waving, the Duke was transported along the canal on a converted barge named in his honour, while the towpath was lined by hundreds of people in their Sunday-best, cheering and waving. In the unlikely event that he had been made aware of Orwell's uncomplimentary description of the people of Wigan, he might have been forgiven for thinking he had been brought to a completely different place.

Orwell's account of Wigan was inconsistent and at times contradictory, designed more to feed his political agenda than for accuracy. While later writing about the new housing estates, early on he seemed to imply that no such improvement plans existed:

> *'In a town like Wigan, for instance, there are over two thousand houses standing which have been condemned for years, and whole sections of the town would be condemned en bloc if there were any hope of other houses being built to replace them.'*

left and below: The Beech Hill council estate, built in the years just before Orwell arrived, has now matured into a leafy suburb – many of the homes now privately owned.

His readership would surely have accepted such statements as reliable – that he was presenting irrefutable proof of a borough ignoring the plight of its residents.

In fact Wigan had not been at all slow off the mark in improving its housing and while vast swathes of the town – particularly around the perimeter of the town centre – very definitely were made up of high density slums, the council had embarked upon a major programme of new 'green-field' estate development almost as soon as the 1924 Housing Act had become law.

After the passing of the more wide-ranging 1936 Housing Act, the council issued demolition orders on whole swathes of sub-standard housing, in and around the town centre, in Scholes, and out to Ince, Pemberton and elsewhere.

With such developments, and the introduction of council-controlled fair rents for these municipal houses, strenuous efforts were being made, albeit perhaps not at the speed many would have liked, to make decent housing

Bamforth's comic postcards were on sale in several north-western holiday resorts, including both Southport and Blackpool. This one probably dates from the late 1930s, and remained on sale throughout the war and long after.

both available and affordable. Even so, Orwell remained far from impressed.

The Beech Hill Estate was the first, with hundreds of houses constructed by the end of the 1920s, at an average cost of £500 each – in those days a not-insignificant sum of money. Many more were erected during the early 1930s.

By the time Orwell arrived in the town, the first phases of the new council estates in Pemberton, Scholes and Whelley had also been completed and, of course, the house-building programme was still on-going. So he did concede that progress was being made but even in doing so, he was somewhat disparaging:

> *'Still, houses* are *being built, and the Corporation building estates, with their row upon row of little red houses, all much liker than two peas (where did that expression come from? Peas have great individuality) are a regular feature of the outskirts of industrial towns.'*

Despite that comment, Orwell did admit that the houses in the Beech Hill estate were well built *'and are quite agreeable to look at'*. Of the council housing in Whelley – which he referred to as Welly – he was rather less impressed.

The quality of many of these properties is evidenced by the fact that they are still occupied today, many now privately owned. Refurbishment has also extended the life of a lot of the late 19th century terraced houses which Orwell so readily denigrated.

That even what he considered to be the poorest of the new council houses were much better than the slums they were built to replace he did not dispute but the irony of a working man and his family being evicted from a condemned house only to be re-housed by the council at nearly twice the rent – albeit now with the luxury of a bathroom and hot and cold running water – did not escape his notice.

Did Orwell do Wigan a disservice? Undoubtedly. But while he may have grossly mis-represented the town, nothing he wrote was untrue – it was simply selective, chosen to further his pre-determined thesis. Was he to blame for the town forever having to carry the enduring burden of that mis-representation? Almost certainly not – or at least not wholly responsible.

The idea of Wigan Pier was already firmly embedded in the British psyche long before Orwell arrived in the town – and it is known that he was initially drawn to the idea of using the town as the epitome of everything that was wrong with Britain's industrial north, because he was confident that 'The Road to Wigan Pier' would make a great book title and one which would certainly resonate with his readers.

Had those miners on the train from Southport not been held up at the Douglas Bank signal box forty years before Orwell ever set foot in the town, and had George Formby never picked up on the idea of Wigan Pier and woven it into his stage act, *The Road to Wigan Pier* would certainly still have been written – it would just have had a much less memorable title and one which would not so easily trip off the tongue today.

Had Orwell's book had a different title, would the town be as well known across the world as it has been now for more than a century? Would there still have been the Bamforth comic postcards which exploited the fact that Wigan was world-famous? Would there still have been a fish and chip shop in Vancouver called 'The Wigan Pier' – or a bar in Tenerife with the same name? Certainly not.

The unanswerable question is how different would Wigan's attitude towards its industrial past have been had the fame of the mythical pier never become an albatross around the town's neck? We will never know.

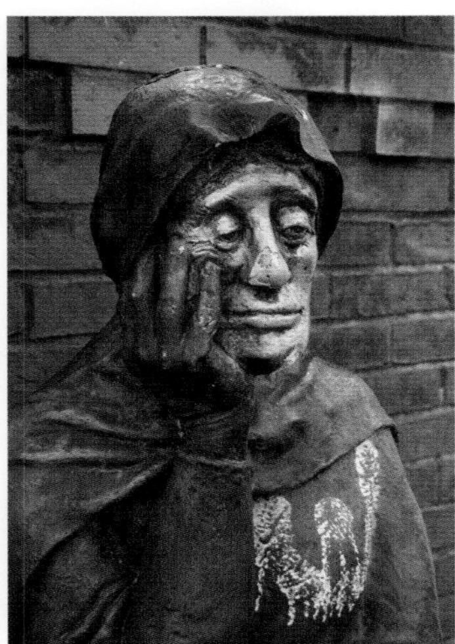

below: The statue of a Wigan pit girl which stands by the decaying remains of the replica pier – the original of which Orwell went in search of in the 1930s – looks suitably fed up with her lot. As part of the regeneration of the pier area, she, too, will be given a face lift.

TODAY AND TOMORROW

THE TWO GEORGES, FORMBY AND ORWELL, would recognise very little of today's Wigan. Westminster Street where the Formbys lived is long gone, as is the Brookers' tripe shop above which Orwell lodged. The sound of clogs on cobbles hasn't been heard for half a century and more, and only the occasional Sunday sounding of the Trencherfield Mill whistle recalls the busy days of the cotton mills.

Wigan once again finds itself in something of a dilemma – how does it continue to develop as a modern town, home to an expanding industrial portfolio, while still paying appropriate homage to the one thing which most people think they know about it?

The town's endeavours to recover from the blight of its post-industrial past have, over the last four decades, been both inventive and largely successful. The once-barren landscapes of colliery spoil heaps and pit yards have been transformed into leisure areas and modern housing developments; wildlife has returned to once-inhospitable wastelands and dinghies now sail on beautifully landscaped flashes.

Around the Wigan Basin and down past the rotting replica of Meyrick Bankes's tippler, plans are afoot for a mixed development of shops and leisure facilities but early

opposite page: Rick Kirby's 2008 *Face of Wigan* is a massive piece of public art which dominates the small area of park bounded by the Wiend, the brutalist 1970s former Civic Centre, and a modern council development of offices and leisure facilities.

below: An artist's impression of what the redeveloped canal area might look like in the future – looking towards the Wigan Basin and Trencherfield Mill.

below: The decaying replica of Meyrick Bankes's pier as it looked in July 2015, just as regeneration work on the area got underway. With negotiations over the complex leases on many of the canalside buildings now resolved, the Council's plans for the area are still being finalised.

press releases and artist's impressions released by Wigan Council show little sign, as yet, of anything designed to perpetuate and enhance the legacy of Wigan Pier.

The area has now been rebranded as 'The Wigan Pier Quarter' and The Wigan Local Plan produced to suggest ways forward. However, it currently says little about the pier's heritage and history, and makes no references to how that heritage is going to be celebrated or enhanced.

The Council's plans, however, while as yet short of detail, clearly do recognise the importance of the pier's legacy as a magnet for drawing people to the area. Councillor David Molyneux, Wigan Council's cabinet member for regeneration is quite clear on that, stating:

> *"While we are in the early stages of our ten year plan for the Wigan Pier Quarter we are clear that the unique history and heritage of Wigan Pier is central to our vision for the quarter's development.*
>
> *We want to seize on the wonderful story that the pier has to tell to create a destination for people to visit, not just from within the borders of Wigan Borough but to attract visitors from Greater Manchester, the North West and across the UK.*
>
> *Part of the development process will involve exploring how best to represent the history and world-renowned fame of the pier. In the wider development of the quarter, significant progress has already been made, including a new community garden, car park at Trencherfield Mill and the impending work on a new 1,000 seat performance venue. As soon as more developments are confirmed we will let people know to make sure the public are kept up-to-date about the revival of this iconic part of Wigan's history."*

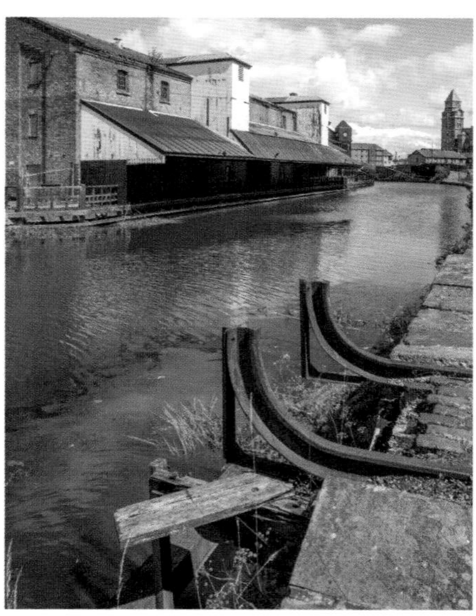

Part of that future exploration will revolve around uses for the buildings which once housed *The Way We Were* and the Orwell pub.

Surely, given the constrained space available in the excellent *Museum of Wigan Life* in the former Waterhouse-designed library and the vast collection of museum artifacts which the Council currently has in store at locations across the borough, a good use for one or other of those buildings would be a museum to Wigan's industrial heritage – not just to 1900, as was the case with *The Way We Were*, but the whole history of Wigan as one of the country's 19th century powerhouses. Look at how the mixture of museums, leisure and shopping helped transform Liverpool's iconic Albert Dock and the area surrounding it.

above: Work progressing on the new car park at Trencherfield Mill, October 2015.

below: Seen from across the canal in April 2016, two lines from Jack Winstanley's '*Ballad of Wigan Pier*' adorn the terracing in the new community garden being developed on the site of the former Pier Nightclub – the first sign that the pier's unique part in Wigan's history might yet live on in the new Wigan Pier Quarter.

This would, of course, require a significant investment but presenting Wigan's history in a fresh way to a new generation could, in this heritage-rich era in which we live, become immensely popular, and once again inspire visitors to explore Wigan and its unlikely pier.

Either of those two currently empty and historic buildings would clearly lend itself to a project like that. A well-structured bid to the Heritage Lottery Fund presenting such a vision could be time and money well spent.

There are, however, few signs so far that the pier's legacy really will be properly celebrated in the area's regeneration. It will take much more than two lines from a song to achieve that. It is to be hoped Wigan Council rises to the challenge.

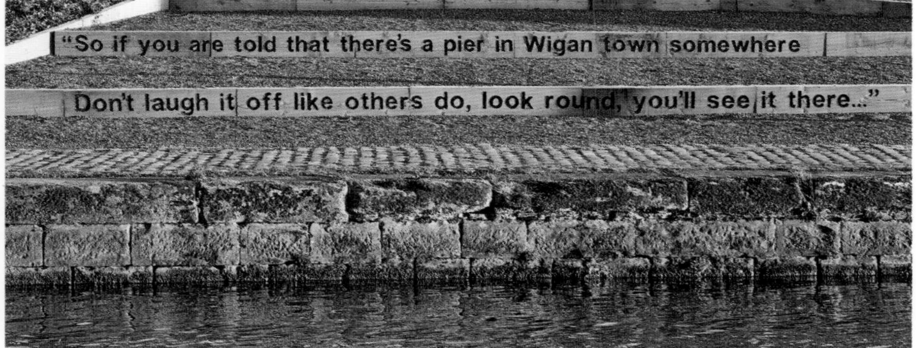

"So if you are told that there's a pier in Wigan town somewhere
Don't laugh it off like others do, look round, you'll see it there..."

FURTHER READING

THERE HAVE BEEN MANY BOOKS written over the years about Wigan, George Orwell, both George Formbys and the history of Music Hall. The following may be of interest.

Anderson, Donald, *Coal – A Pictorial History of the British Coal Industry*, Newton Abbot: David & Charles, 1982
Anderson, Donald & France, A.A., *Wigan Coal and Iron*, Wigan: Smiths Books, 1994
Armstrong, Stephen, *The Road to Wigan Pier Revisited*, London: Constable, 2012
Baker, Richard Anthony, *British Music Hall - an Illustrated History*, Barnsley: Pen & Sword Books, 2014
Blakeman, Bob, *Wigan: A Historical Souvenir*, Stroud: Sutton Publishing, 1996
Bret, David, *George Formby - A Troubled Genius*, London: Robson Books, 2001 (revised re-issue through Lulu.com 2014)
Collis, Robert *George Orwell - English Rebel*, Oxford: Oxford University Press 2013
Davies, Alan, *The Pit Brow Women of the Wigan Coalfield*, Stroud: The History Press, 2002
Davies, Alan, and Hudson, Len, *The Wigan Coalfield*, Stroud: The History Press, 1999
Hannavy, John, *Edwardian Mining in Old Postcards*, Wellington: PiXZ, 2013
Hannavy, John, *Historic Wigan*, Preston: Carnegie Press, 1990
Hannavy, John, *Wigan History & Guide*, Stroud: The History Press, 2008
Hannavy, John & Winstanley, Jack, *Wigan Pier - An Illustrated History*, Wigan: Smiths Books, 1985
Hilton, John, *Wigan Town and Country Rambles*, Wigan: Caxton Press, 1934
Major, John, *My Old Man, a Personal History of Music Hall*, London: William Collins, 2013
Orwell, George, *Down and Out in Paris and London*, London: Penguin Classics, 2001
Orwell, George, *The Road to Wigan Pier*, London: Penguin Classsics, 2001
Sheldon, Michael, *George Orwell: The Authorised Biography*, London: William Heinemann, 1991
Stuart, Charles Douglas, *The Variety Stage; A History of the Music Halls from the Earliest Period to the Present Time*, London: T. Fisher Unwin, 1895
Smart, Sue & Howard, Richard Bothway, *It's Turned out Nice Again* Ely: Melrose Books, 2011

INDEX